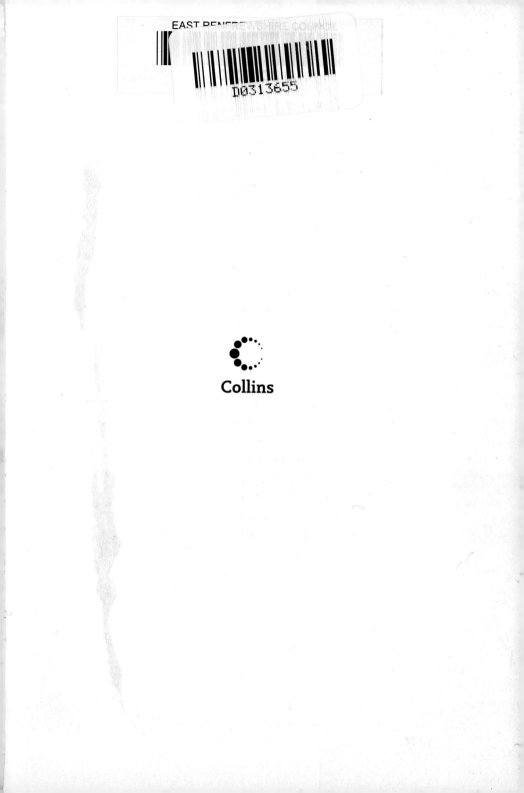

Collins

need to know?

Whiskies

Dominic Roskrow

Collins

First published in 2008 by Collins
an imprint of
HarperCollins Publishers
77–85 Fulham Palace Road
London W6 8JB

www.collins.co.uk

Collins is a registered trademark of
HarperCollins Publishers Limited

10 09 08
6 5 4 3 2 1

A catalogue record for this book is available from
the British Library

Dominic Roskrow hereby asserts his moral right to
be identified as the author of this work.

This book was produced by Blue Island Publishing for
HarperCollins Publishers Ltd.

Editor: Michael Ellis
Designer: Stephen Bere
Series design: Mark Thomson
Front cover photograph: © Images
Back cover photographs: Photographer

ISBN-13: 978-0-00-726164-2
ISBN-10: 0-00-726164-0

Every effort was made to ensure that information
contained in the book was correct at the time of
going to press. However, visiting details can change,
and it is recommended that readers always phone
ahead before visiting any distillery.

Printed and bound by Printing Express Ltd,
Hong Kong

Contents

Introduction   6

1   **Debunking the whisky myths**   8

2   **Types of whisky** 14

3   **The magic of malt** 26

4   **Nosing and tasting whisky** 38

5   **Buying whisky** 44

6   **Scotland's distilleries** 52

7   **The fabulous fifty** 138

8   **Irish whiskey** 150

9   **American whiskey** 160

10   **The rest of the world** 170

11   **Independent bottlers** 178

Glossary 184

Need to know more? 188

Index 190

Introduction

There is no other alcoholic spirit quite like whisky. No other spirit commands such dedication, interest and affection – has magazines written exclusively about it, clubs formed in its honour and festivals established around the world to celebrate it. And no other spirit has spawned its very own tourist industry.

The pot stills at Highland Park Distillery

It's a matter of character

Whisky, in all its many guises but particularly as a single malt, has a personality that no other drink, including wine and beer, can quite match. Mystery and magic are hidden in its golden depths, and myriad flavours mark it apart from any other drink. Russell Andersen, distillery manager at Highland Park, on Orkney, perhaps puts it best:

"Whisky is black magic or a miracle, depending on your religious standpoint," he says. "Each malt contains a unique set of flavours and each cask acts in a slightly different way. Scientists can analyse and explain some of it, but no-one knows it all and no-one can predict how any one cask will react. It retains a mystery and because of that, a special appeal."

There's something else, too. In these homogenised and globalised times, when, no matter where you are in the world, you'll recognise most of the drinks in the bar, individual whiskies can't be duplicated. They have a provenance, each one coming from a specific area or country, and in the case of single malts, from a particular distillery. And often that distillery is nothing more than a glorified cow barn and a warehouse or two. It doesn't get more localised than that. One sip and you're transported to a remote glen in the Highlands, or a rugged west coast island.

A mystique has grown up around whisky, and its thousands of different manifestations can make it a daunting subject to approach as a novice. This shouldn't be the case, as whisky is, in fact, a very simple drink, containing only grain, water and yeast.

Sampling whisky from the cask at Glenfiddich Distillery

Dawn of a golden age

These are exciting times for whisky. Huge new distilleries are being built by Diageo and William Grant, new independent distilleries are springing up on Islay and in Speyside, and more people than ever before are becoming interested in the subject. That's where this book comes in. Its purpose is to provide a pathway through the whisky maze, to demystify it, and to provide the platform from which a lifetime's hobby can be launched.

Although, initially, the world of whisky may seem to be governed by convention and regulation, it is, in fact, one of individualism and free expression. Its makers are constantly seeking out new ways to make this wonderful spirit even better. Be aware, though: whisky is for life. No matter which way the bug gets you – as a collector, taster or distillery visitor – it'll never go away. It will provide you with years of happiness, introduce you to scores of like-minded people, have you salivating over the latest distillery releases and result in long trainspotter-like conversations about the properties of Spanish oak compared to American.

The world of whisky is a warm, welcoming, weird and wonderful one. Welcome to the club!

must know

Whisky is a very simple drink. It contains only grain, some water and yeast. Add anything else and it's no longer whisky, or at least, not under the terms laid down by the largest trading zones.

Charring casks prior to use in the Macallan cooperidge

1 Debunking the whisky myths

Mention whisky to most people and they will immediately think of Scotland. Push it a bit further and, chances are, they will know that it is divided between single malt whiskies, which are special and premium, and blends – the "cheap and nasty stuff". Given the ubiquity of whisky, its contribution to the global economy, and its importance to the heritage not just of Scotland but also of Ireland and America, a surprisingly small amount is known about it.

Whisky lore

It may be a popular drink, but whisky is also one that engenders more than a little reverence. Alongside this due respect for a fine drink, however, a few too many myths and fallacies have grown up about what's "right" and "wrong". So, before we go any further, let's debunk a few of the worst offenders.

Whisky is a truly international drink, enjoyed around the world.

Its traditions make whisky very much a convivial drink.

Enjoying whisky

There will be few ground rules in this book, but the first and most important is that there is no right way of appreciating and enjoying whisky. It's the ultimate bespoke drink – wear it any way that suits you. And if anyone tells you that you should add water to it, you shouldn't add water to it, you shouldn't add ice, you should drink it standing on one leg ... then politely tell them that this is a drink for individuals.

The blender's art

Most of this book will be concerned with single malt whisky because malt distilleries provide so many routes to explore and so many different flavours to discover. But it's worth bearing in mind that, although the demand for single malts is growing, blended whisky still accounts for about 19 out of every 20 glasses of whisky consumed – and there are very good reasons for this.

Blended whisky is tainted with a poor reputation because, frankly, a good proportion of it is rubbish. The average blend is made up of some malt whiskies mixed together and blended with a whisky made from another grain. Often this is mass-produced grain whisky with a fairly neutral taste, and it is added in large quantities, reducing the flavour of the malt. Often the grain is matured in tired old casks for the legal minimum time. So, throw together high proportions of cheaply-made grain whisky and a proportion of second grade malt and you get the sort of cheap blends you find in small supermarkets, often with preposterously contrived Scottish-sounding names, such as Glen Kilt and Heather Bagpipe Macbeth Deluxe Scotch.

It doesn't have to be this way, and some of the most sophisticated and satisfying whiskies in the world are premium Scotch blended whiskies. They are some of the most expensive, too.

We deal with blended whisky more fully in the next chapter, but suffice to say here that the skill of a master blender is one of the greatest of artisanal skills, and it is a great mistake to dismiss blends as being in any way inferior to single malts. Many blends use only the finest malt whisky in relatively large proportions, blended with top quality grain whisky produced in the finest oak casks.

Chivas Regal 18-year-old blended whisky

must know

A great blender uses his nose to help him form an orchestra of flavours and to balance different styles of whisky to produce the oral equivalent of classical music to stunning effect.

The art of blending, as carried out at Compass Box

Casks of maturing Irish whiskey at Cooley Distillery

Suntory Distillery in Japan makes use of a wide variety of pot stills.

Beyond Scotland

When it comes to whisky, it simply isn't true that Scotland is the only great producing nation. The sheer scale of whisky production in Scotland, the large number of distilleries and the exacting quality controls on whisky production ensure that, should a definitive list of the world's best whiskies be drawn up, it would be dominated by Caledonia.

But on such a hypothetical list there would be many other distinctive whiskies from around the world. A few American bourbons, a smattering of Irish whiskeys, and a number of Japanese and Canadian whiskies would not only be on the list, but would also be vying for the top spots.

Old, rare and expensive

Don't fall into the trap of thinking that older whisky is always better, and that whisky has to be expensive to be good. Although whisky becomes rarer and therefore more expensive after 20 years, it doesn't necessarily improve. The influence of the cask can begin to take over, and, just as with the flavour of oak in wine, it's not to everybody's taste.

Some whiskies are more robust than others and cope well with the wood. They may taste fine after 25 years of ageing, and even beyond 30 or 40 years. Such whiskies are, however, few and far between. Other malts are submerged by oak much younger. So while whiskies aged for more than 25 years will require a serious investment financially, it's a moot point as to whether you'd want to drink them.

The flip side to this argument is, of course, that some whisky styles actually benefit from youthfulness, and are better drunk younger. The bottom line is that you don't need to break the bank to enjoy outstanding whisky. We may all get the chance to taste a rare and old malt now and again, but, with only a modest amount of exploration and investigation, the whisky enthusiast is likely to rapidly build up a personal repertoire of value-for-money malts, undoubtedly including one or two reserved for the top shelf and that special occasion.

Maker's Mark bourbon opts for the Scottish spelling of "whisky".

You say "whisky", I say "whiskey"

Finally, a word about the spelling: "whisky" or "whiskey". The word is an anglicised bastardisation of the Gaelic *uisge beatha* ("water of life") – words claimed from a language common to old Scotland and old Ireland. The Scots opt for the former spelling, the Irish favour the latter, with the "e".

Once again, there can be no right or wrong in this debate, and outside these two countries both spellings can be – and are – used. In America "whiskey" is the more common spelling, though several producers, including Maker's Mark, choose to spell the word without the "e". Japan goes with the Scottish way, as does Canada.

must know

As a very basic rule of thumb, single malt whisky reaches maturity from seven years onwards, and a 10 to 12-year-old would represent a premium malt. Up to about 20 years, it could be argued that the whisky will continue to improve. After that, though, all bets are off.

2 Types of whisky

Push most people and, chances are, they would know of two different whisky styles: single malt and blended whisky. There are actually four styles of whisky made in Scotland, and, contrary to popular belief, single malt whisky is not the only one that produces a top-drawer product. All four do. However, this book does mainly concern itself with single malt whisky for the reason that malt manifests itself in so many different ways, and is, therefore, the most intriguing of not just the four styles of whisky, but also of all spirits of any kind.

Whisky classifications

Although this book's primary focus is on malt whisky, it would be remiss of any book about the subject of whisky not to make at least some reference to the other styles of whisky produced in Scotland and in other parts of the world.

Malted barley is here being turned by hand at Bowmore Distillery, which is one of the few distilleries still to have these kind of floor maltings.

Malt whisky

Malt whisky is produced in batches, using only malted barley, yeast and water. The whole process of making malt whisky, from the malting of the barley through to maturation of the spirit, is covered in detail in the next chapter *(see pp26–35)*. Put simply, however, the process involves fermenting malted barley and water into a wash, or strong beer, which is then distilled in a pot still; the resulting spirit is collected and matured in oak casks.

Malted barley isn't the only grain that can make whisky, and nor is the batch method the only way of distilling the wash. It is, however, the grain that ferments easiest with yeast because of the richness of the sugars it releases; it also produces the most flavoursome alcohol.

Grain whisky

Whisky can be produced from a range of grains, including unmalted barley, corn, wheat and rye. These grains are always mixed with an amount of malted barley to ensure successful fermentation.

The fundamental difference between malt whisky and whiskies made with grains other than malt is that malt is made in batches, whereas other grain whisky production doesn't need to be. It can be made in a continuous, factory-like process.

The continuous, or column, still was originally invented by a Scotsman, Robert Stein, but perfected by an Irishman called Aeneas Coffey. It is after him that the Coffey Still is named. This is ironic really, because it was adopted in Scotland and rejected by the Irish, who felt it would undermine their traditional way of making whisky, and who in turn lost their world dominance in whisky because of it.

Unlike the pleasantly curvy copper pot still, the column still is a workmanlike, no-nonsense piece of industrial equipment. Whisky is made in it by pouring fermented wash down a series of tall columns and against steam at extremely high temperature and pressure. The liquid is vaporised and then passed against a series of plates where it is condensed into liquid. Whereas malt comes off the still as a fruity, appley fresh spirit, grain spirit is considerably stronger and smells like soggy, slightly sweet breakfast cereal in hot milk. The spirit it produces has far less taste than single malt, and is referred to in some countries as neutral grain spirit.

The process allows spirit to be produced in large quantities relatively quickly, and it was the use of grain whisky in creating blended whisky that turned Scotch into the worldwide success story it is today.

Single grain whisky

Grain whisky is bound by similar laws to single malt, and, in Scotland, that means it must be matured for a minimum of three years in oak casks. Almost all of it goes into blended whisky and very little is bottled as grain whisky in its own right. Generally speaking,

This column still at Kittling Ridge, in the USA is built for small-batch production; larger stills of this kind can be several storeys high.

Cameron Bridge Distillery produces grain whisky for blending and single grain bottlings.

"Cameron Brig" single grain whisky

this is just as well, as some grain whisky is matured in old casks that don't impact positively on the whisky. However, there are subtle differences between the grains produced by the different distilleries in Scotland, and even more significant differences between the whiskies produced by each type of grain. Notable examples exist of single grain whiskies that have been aged in high quality casks for many years and, as a result, have become very tasty and absorbing. They take on many of the characteristics of the oak cask and, because there are no other dominant flavours in the spirit itself, the end result can be highly attractive.

"A grain whisky is like a blank canvas," says Euan Shand, managing director of whisky company Duncan Taylor, which sells a range of outstanding grain whiskies. "Over the years the cask leaves its mark on the whisky and this can be outstanding."

A growing number of enthusiasts share Euan's view, and today single grain whiskies are enjoying their time in the spotlight. An additional appeal of single grain whiskies is that they are good value.

Blended whisky

Single malt is to whisky what foreign language films are to cinema – loved by a limited number of enthusiasts, but something of an acquired taste. Blended whisky is the drink version of Hollywood – produced on a huge scale, predictable, and often bland and unexciting, but with a sizeable smattering of true classics.

Blended whisky is a mix of malt whiskies with whisky made from another grain. When made properly, it is a full orchestra – a sophisticated blend of different instruments combined with care and skill to make a perfect harmony for the taste-buds.

Bell's 8-year-old blended whisky

must know

About 95% of whisky sold, or 19 out of every 20 glasses, is blended whisky. It is the most palatable of all Scotch whisky styles – indeed it was designed to be that way – and it is the type of Scotch that introduces most drinkers to the pleasures of whisky.

Particularly in Scotland, grain distilleries, such as Cameron Bridge, tend to be more industrial in scale and appearance than the more artisanal malt distilleries.

Whyte & Mackay Special, a blended whisky without an age statement

Glenturret is the home of The Famous Grouse and supplies some of the malt whisky in its blend.

The quality of blends

Let's dispel a few of the fallacies about blends. They are not necessarily inferior to single malts, nor do they have to be blander and less interesting. Quite the opposite, in fact. When a blend is well put together, it contains a vast array of styles and flavours, and requires a developed palate to appreciate it. Quality blends can cost considerably more than most malts and can contain rare and old whisky.

The image problem that blends have is caused by two factors: the first is that they can contain poor quality grain whisky, matured for the minimum period of three years in poor quality casks; the second is that the proportion of grain whisky to malt can be very high, resulting in an anaemic blend.

The whole point of blended whisky is to create a consistent product, so that, wherever and whenever the customer buys it, the whisky will taste the same. But, because each cask of whisky tastes slightly different to the next, over time the mix of whiskies in a blend will change. A great deal of effort is made to replicate the exact flavour profile of the blend.

Secret recipes

Distillers don't want customers to think their blends are changing, so whisky makers tend not to disclose which whiskies go into their blends. So, how can you spot a good blend without tasting it?

The simplest advice is to seek out the best known blends. The big names of blended whisky tend to have attained their position for a very good reason. The likes of Bell's, Famous Grouse, Dewar's, Whyte & Mackay and Teacher's are mainstream blends, but they are made with very good quality malt whisky from some of the most respected distilleries in Scotland.

Look also for an age on the label. Some blended whiskies state an age in the same way as single malts do. And, just as with single malts, the age refers to the youngest whisky in the mix, and applies equally to the malt and the grain content.

On pages 147-48, I have listed a personal selection of great blended whiskies.

Johnnie Walker Green Label, a brand of blended malt whisky

Blended malt whiskies

A single malt whisky is a whisky made from the product of one distillery and it has a taste distinctive to that distillery. But each one is a solo instrumentalist and, it could be argued, lacks the subtlety and sophistication of some other styles of whisky.

The small ensemble of the whisky world is the category known as "vatted malt whisky", or increasingly "blended malt whisky". This is a harmonious blend of single malts from different distilleries. A vatted malt whisky may include anything from three different malt whiskies to a couple of dozen, but the mix contains only malt.

must know

To find a perfect balance of flavours between the warring whiskies in a blended malt takes considerable skill and effort. But often blended malts are cheaper than single malts, and so they offer excellent value for money. My recommendations are listed on page 149.

This is the category that offers Scotch the best opportunity to appeal to a younger generation and to find a place in style bars. Because vatted whiskies are the product of several distilleries, they are not restrained by any traditional baggage and can adopt zany and genre-breaking names, such as Sheep Dip and Monkey Shoulder.

In the last few years, the Scotch whisky industry has replaced the term "vatted malt" with the less industrial-sounding "blended malt". This is not to be confused with "blended whisky".

Other whiskies around the world

As well as Scotch malt, grain, blended whisky and blended malt, many other styles of whisky have been developed in various parts of the world, most notably in Ireland, America, Canada and Japan.
Here's a round-up of the most distinguished types.

Irish pot still whiskey

If Irish whiskey has fallen off the radar for many people, then it only has itself to blame. As whisky enthusiasts have demonstrated an endless thirst for more knowledge, the few remaining distillers in Ireland have done little to meet this challenge. And while the Scotch Whisky Association has fought tirelessly to define what constitutes the different types of Scotch whisky, the Irish have been guilty of letting confusion reign. Worst of all, they have devalued one of the world's great whisky styles: Irish pot still whiskey.

Contrary to what some might tell you, Irish pot still whiskey is not simply whiskey made in Ireland in a pot still; it is much more than that. The uniqueness

Redbreast 12-year-old pure pot still Irish whiskey

of pot still whiskey is that it is made using both malted and unmalted barley, with unmalted barley normally being the main component. The resulting whiskey is oilier than Scottish malt whisky. It is normally, but not necessarily, triple distilled to produce a smoother, rounder and fruitier spirit than single malt. While pot still whiskey goes into many Irish blends, there are just two great pot still whiskeys bottled in their own right – the young-ish Green Spot, and the rich, heavy Redbreast.

Blended Irish whiskey

At its best, blended Irish whiskey is also unique. Brands such as Paddys and Powers have a traditional pot still whiskey taste but are softened by the addition of grain whiskey produced in a column still.

Powers Gold Label blended Irish whiskey

Bourbon

Bourbon is an American whiskey and adheres to the rule that the spirit must be a mix of grain, yeast and water. Bourbon is made with a mix of grains, of which at least 51 per cent must be corn. Other grains that might be used are malted and unmalted barley, wheat and rye. The mix is fermented by yeast and then distilled in a continuous column still. There are other technical definitions pertaining to heat and alcoholic strength, but after distillation the new spirit must be matured in new charred oak barrels for a minimum of two years.

Bourbon takes its name from Bourbon County in Kentucky, and most of it is produced by Kentucky distilleries, such as Jim Beam, Four Roses and Woodford Reserve. However, it can be made in any part of the United States.

Jim Beam Black bourbon whiskey   **Four Roses small batch bourbon**

Tennessee whiskey

Jack Daniel's is sometimes mistaken for a bourbon but is in fact a Tennessee whiskey. Essentially, it is made in the same way as bourbon, but with the addition of an extra procedure, known as the Lincoln County Process. This process entails pouring the new make spirit through a wall of Maple charcoal before putting it into the barrel. This filters out impurities and, according to its producers, makes for a smoother and more rounded finished whiskey.

Rye whiskey

The mash bill – the mix of grains – in an American whiskey can vary, and so it's perfectly possible to make whiskey in which corn isn't the dominant grain (as it mostly is in the US). Rye whiskey must be made up of at least 51 per cent rye, but the proportion can be considerably more. As a style, it was once a big player, but it fell out of favour and became something of a rarity. That's changing again, though, as adventurous drinkers seek out big and bold flavours once more. Rye whiskey can be made with malted or unmalted rye. At its best, it is big, oily and spicy – and unforgettable too.

Jack Daniel's Tennessee Whiskey

Rittenhouse Rye 21-year-old whisky

Japanese whisky

In simplistic terms, anyone considering producing whisky must decide between two paths: to copy the Scottish way, or to try and find a new approach within the existing rules. Traditionally, Japan's whisky was an imitation of that from Scotland. Japan's approach to whisky making was rather like their approach to the car industry: they came, they copied and they perfected.

Hanyu Single Cask No. 1 malt whisky

Fuji-Gotemba 18-year-old single malt

For many years now, Japan has produced technically perfect, and occasionally outstanding, malt whiskies. However, in the last few years, competition judges have noticed a distinctive and unique characteristic to Japanese single malt. It is an earthy, slightly mushroomy flavour, and something of an acquired taste – whisky's answer to unpasteurised blue cheese. But, when it is integrated into some of the better, wonderfully balanced Japanese offerings, it is sublime. For this reason, it increasingly sets Japanese whisky apart as a style all of its own.

Forty Creek Barrel Select blended whisky

Canadian Club 10-year-old blended whisky

Canadian whisky

Often referred to as rye, Canadian whisky is far removed from the battering ram rye product made in the USA. In most cases, it is actually a sophisticated blend of several different rye whiskies mixed with a more neutral grain whisky. Canadian whisky may also contain 9.09 per cent of some other flavouring, such as bourbon or fruit juice.

Canadian whisky is often dismissed as bland, but at its best it is a sophisticated, nuanced and subtle blend of flavours.

want to know more?

further reading
• The Complete Guide to Whisky by Jim Murray
• Malt Whisky by Charles MacLean and Jason Lowe
• Handbook of Whisky by Dave Broom

websites
www.whiskymag.com
www.maltadvocate.com

The setting of Japan's Miyagikyo Distillery

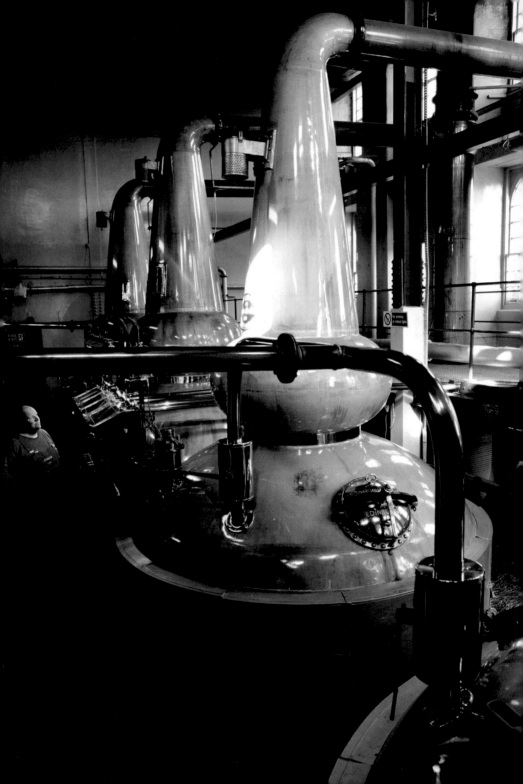

3 The magic of malt

Single malt whisky is the type of whisky most closely associated with Scotland, and is the spirit produced by the vast majority of its 100 or so distilleries. Although the raw materials used in the production process are pretty much identical at every malt distillery, no two malts taste exactly the same. This is the mystery of malt: how three basic ingredients treated in so similar a way can yet produce such a panoply of flavours. As we shall see, though, there are a large number of variables that will affect the final outcome of the whisky.

What is single malt whisky?

Malt whisky is made using just malted barley, yeast and water, and the word "single" refers to the fact that it comes from just one distillery. It does not mean that the whisky is the product of a single cask, and a bottle of single malt will normally be made from a mix of whiskies from a large number of different casks.

must know

Distilleries produce malt whiskies for two purposes: to bottle as single malt, and to provide stock for mixing into blended whisky. Not all distilleries do both, but if a distillery does sell some of its output as a single malt then in all likelihood it will have a core range of styles. For instance, it might bottle a younger, standard version, a medium-aged one, and an older one. The owners of the distillery will seek consistency in each type, so that a customer buying a bottle at any time and in any country will know what to expect.

Casks and batches

The wooden casks in which whisky is matured may be of different sizes, different types of oak and may have previously contained a range of other drinks. They may also be of different ages. As we shall see, the age on the label of a bottle of whisky does not necessarily mean all the whisky in the bottle is that age. In fact, this is highly unlikely. Single malt whisky is made in batches. So a proportion of yeast, barley and water is used in each batch to create a quantity of malt whisky in one go, and the spirit produced is then stored in oak casks to mature in warehouses for years. When the initial production process is finished, the distiller must start again from scratch.

As single malt whisky is made in batches and because each cask of whisky is slightly different to the next, the distiller has to choose a mix of casks to meet the whisky's specific taste characteristics; the choice is made by assessing cask samples.

In addition to its core range, a distillery may issue a smaller quantity of special bottles. This may be to mark a special occasion, to make use of a special cask, or even simply to meet the demands for rare and expensive whiskies in the collectors' market.

Making malt whisky: fermentation

• The first stage of making malt whisky is to take the three basic raw ingredients of malted barley, yeast and water, and to make beer with them.

• Malted barley is barley that has been "tricked" into growing. To do this, the barley is soaked in warm water and left to germinate. After a while, the cell walls of the grain will be broken down and a shoot will start to grow. The traditional way of doing this is to lay the malt out on large floors, though only a handful of distilleries still have such floor maltings. The more common practice today is for distilleries to buy malt in from commercial maltsters, who carry out the process in automated systems.

• Germination releases starches and enzymes. The starches will become the sugars required to make alcohol, and the enzymes enable this process to occur.

• Germination has to be halted before it goes too far and destroys the starches. This is achieved by heating the germinating barley. Malt is spread out on a metal

must know
There are three stages to making malt whisky: fermentation, which effectively means making beer; distillation, which separates the spirit from the water; and maturation.

The malting floor at Balvenie Distillery

Kilning barley with peat at Balvenie Distillery

Malt being ground in a Porteus mill at Glen Garioch Distillery

A stainless-steel mash tun at Glen Garioch Distillery

floor above a furnace and dried by heat applied either directly from the furnace or indirectly by air that is passed through the malt after being heated by oil or steam radiators.

• It is during this kilning process that the malt may be dried by smoke from burning peat. The flavour imparted to the barley in this process will remain with it throughout fermentation and distillation, and will influence the final spirit, giving it the phenolic, smoky and medicinal characteristics that are the hallmarks of certain malts.

• When the drying process is finished, the malt is ground in a mill (most often made by Yorkshire company Porteus) into a rough flour. This in turn is mixed with hot water in a mashing machine and then passed into a large holding vessel made of cast iron or stainless steel, known as a mash tun.

• The process at this stage is a little bit like making a pot of tea with tea leaves. Hot water is passed through the grain up to three times and this flushes out the enzymes and sugars required to make alcohol. The brown, non-alcoholic liquid – known as worts – passes out through the perforated bottom of the mash tun where it is collected and cooled. When the grain has been exhausted of all its nutrients, it is collected and sent off to be used as cattle feed.

• The worts are transferred into another vessel – often made of wood but increasingly these days stainless steel – where yeast is added and fermentation takes place. This process is the same as making beer, except that the fermentation isn't carried out in sterile conditions.

• The yeast effectively eats the sugars created by the starch and enzymes in the malt, producing alcohol and carbon dioxide. The process takes upwards of 50 hours and produces a sharp and sour beer due to the secondary fermentation provoked by bacteria. The result is a distiller's beer – known as wash. It has a strength of 5% to 9% abv (alcohol by volume), and this solution is now ready for distillation.

Old-fashioned wooden wash backs at Aultmore Distillery

Making malt whisky: distillation

• Most but not all single malt whisky is distilled twice, in large copper kettles known as pot stills. Distillation is the process of heating the solution to boil off a variety of alcohols – all of which have different boiling points – and collecting the ones the distiller wants by separating them out and condensing them back from gas to liquid.

• The first distillation takes place in the wash still. The still is heated, the vapours rise and pass up the copper still towards the tapered neck, then pass down a tube known as the lyne arm, where they are cooled in a condenser by cold water passing over the outside of the copper. The first distillation passes through the spirits safe into a receiving tank, known as the low wines or feints receiver.

• The liquid – known as low wines – will have an alcoholic strength of just over 20% abv. To prepare it

must know
The first alcohols to boil off in the second distillation are at best foul tasting and at worst poisonous, so for the first part of the run the spirit is condensed and stored in a separate tank. This rejected portion is very strong and is known as the heads or foreshots. It will go back to the feints receiver and be mixed with the next wash for a fresh distillation.

The role of copper

The distiller's decision to make the cut and save the spirit – and it may be as little as 10 or 12 per cent of the total run – will have a huge influence on how the saved spirit (called new make spirit, and with an alcoholic strength usually in the high 60s) will taste. The original raw ingredients used, the length of fermentation, and the speed with which the spirit passes through the still will all have a major influence on the taste of the spirit.

The copper stills have a huge role to play in the character of the whisky too. Copper has a very rough surface and, as the spirit vapours pass over it, the metal will detain and remove impurities such as sulphur. The spirit is made up of hundreds of fats and impurities, which are known as congeners. These provide flavours, both positive and negative, and the more of them that are removed, the lighter the nature of the finished spirit. Big, tall stills hold back a greater proportion of the flavour compounds, while short squat stills allow more through, resulting in a meatier, more robust and heavy spirit.

Every distillery's stills are different, and their form will help define the characteristics of that distillery's whisky. More than that, the history, culture and economic development of different regions of Scotland have helped to influence the sort of stills generally to be found in different places, helping to define traditional regional styles.

for the second distillation, it is mixed with the stronger, rejected spirits (the foreshots) from the previous distillation run, giving it an alcoholic strength of about 28% abv.

• It is from the second distillation that the distiller will collect his final spirit, and so this time around he must carefully monitor the spirit and separate out the proportion of the run that will adversely affect the taste of the final alcohol.

• When the moment is right, the distiller will transfer the flowing spirit to a different holding tank. This spirit (known as "new make") will be kept to make whisky; it forms the middle section, or heart of the run. The longer the run continues, the weaker the spirit will become, and once more the distiller must decide when the "cut" is complete. At this point, he must transfer the flowing spirit into a third tank, where the rest of the run (known as tails or feints) is rejected and passed back for the next distillation.

Traditional copper pot stills at Craigellachie Distillery

Making malt whisky: maturation

New make spirit is clear and strong. It is characterised by estery flavours (young, yeasty, cereally), strong fruit flavours (often green apples), liquorice and – in the case of whisky made using peated malt – a dense wood bonfire taste and smell. Water will be added to it to bring it down to its casking strength, normally 63.5%. It is then put into oak casks.

New make spirit at Knockdhu Distillery

Under Scottish law, spirit can be described as whisky only after it has been matured in oak casks for a minimum of three years. There is, however, considerable scope for flexibility when it comes to the sort of cask used, and this too will have a major impact on the whisky that the cask will produce.

The cooperage at Balvenie Distillery

must know

Casks are made from oak that is at least 80 years old. The oak is cut into narrow strips known as staves, which are seasoned to dry out for up to two years. The casks are constructed and then toasted, or charred, on the inside to release vanillins and other flavour compounds.

By far the highest proportion of casks are made of American oak, but a significant proportion are made of European oak. European casks are about 10 times as expensive as American barrels, but some distilleries make the outlay because they say it is essential to maintain the distinct nature of their whisky.

New oak casks would be too powerful for malt whisky, and so in the vast majority of cases (although there are exceptions) malt whisky is matured in casks that have been used for something else previously, most commonly bourbon or sherry. What the cask has contained before will, of course, greatly influence the flavour of the malt inside.

The mystery of casks

It is in the casks that the real magic of malt takes place. Casks come in various sizes, and include barrels (180 litres), hogsheads (250 litres), puncheons (450 litres) and butts (500 litres). Smaller casks, such as quarter casks, are occasionally used, and their size really does matter. The reason for this is that the smaller the cask, the more liquid inside the container can come into contact with the wood, and therefore the more influence the wood can have on the whisky. Temperature is an intrinsic part of this, too, and Scotland's damp and cold climate ensures a stately and gentle maturation, lasting years. Wood imparts colour and taste to the whisky. As the liquid warms and expands it will be forced into the wood. As it cools it contracts and comes out of the wood again, drawing with it colour and flavour. But there are two other reactions at this stage: the whisky will leave some fats and impurities in the wood, so the wood effectively removes some flavours too; and the wood and the whisky will react with each other to create whole new flavours.

Maturing whisky casks at Glenfiddich

The life of a cask

The more times the cask is used to make whisky, the more tired the wood will become and the less effective it will be in adding flavour. So when whisky is added to a cask for the first time (known as the first fill), the influence of sherry or bourbon will be at its strongest; the second time less so. A sample taken after, say, five years from a first fill sherry cask will be significantly darker than a five year-old sample from a second fill, and it will have a much richer and stronger sherry smell to it too.

Eventually the cask becomes too tired to be used any more. How long the whisky remains in the cask is up to the whisky maker, but each cask is monitored carefully. Over long periods, the flavour from the oak may start to overpower the malt.

The angels' share

Another consideration is alcoholic strength. Each year, a small amount of spirit evaporates from the cask (known as the "angels' share") and the strength of the whisky consequently declines a little. This must be monitored: if the strength falls below 40% abv, the spirit can no longer be described as whisky.

After three years in the cask, the spirit can legally be called whisky, and at some point after that it will complete its maturation and be removed from the cask for bottling or blending. If you take into consideration the time it took to grow the wood used for the cask, it's a journey that might have taken more than 130 years.

want to know more?
further reading
• **The Complete Book of Whisky by Jim Murray**
• **The Making of Scotch Whisky by Michael Moss and John Hume**
• **Malt Whisky by Charles MacLean and Jason Lowe**
• **Scotland and its Whiskies by Michael Jackson**

Scotland's whisky regions

Scotland is three nations in one – Highlands, Lowlands and Islands – and each has its own history, culture, economy and personality. In whisky terms, these regions have traditionally been broken down further, with two sub-regions to each.

General characteristics

The regions have been used in the past as a convenient way of making some sweeping generalisations about the character of the whisky from each region. Lowland malts, for instance, tend to be produced on big commercial stills, built to meet the demand for malts to mix into blends and to export through the ports of Glasgow and Leith. These tall stills make light, floral styles of whisky. Highland whiskies were often produced illegally, and the stills were small so they could be hidden or moved. Small squat stills allow heavier flavours to pass into the distillation, so Highland whiskies are generally considered heavier, richer and more flavoursome than Lowland whiskies.

We shouldn't get too hung up with these sorts of generalisations, which at best are over-simplistic and at worst do a considerable disservice to the many distilleries that operate outside accepted conventions. Such classifications are only important in so much as they are frequently used on the bottle labels to act as a rough guide to the style of spirit within.

Increasingly, though, whisky makers are turning convention on its head and experimenting with different tastes and styles, irrespective of the area from which they come. This trend will be exacerbated in the near future. William Grant has opened its new malt distillery at Girvan, in the southwest of Scotland, and is producing a malt that may have a similar taste profile to that produced at its Balvenie Distillery in the heart of Speyside.

The six regions

Lowlands
Many of the distilleries from this region are now closed, but
Auchentoshan at the western edge of Glasgow, Glenkinchie to
the east of Edinburgh and Bladnoch in the southeast towards
the border with England are included.

Campbeltown
Once rich with distilleries, the Campbeltown area now has just
three: the "three for the price of one" Springbank Distillery,
where Springbank, Hazelburn and Longrow are produced;
Glengyle, which opened in 2004 and held a party in 2007 to
celebrate the coming of age of its first whisky; and the semi-
operational Glen Scotia Distillery.

Highlands
Stretching from Glengoyne just north of Glasgow to Pulteney in
Wick in the far northeast – but excluding the area between
Aberdeen and Inverness in the east – the Highlands is a vast
region and covers a diverse array of whisky styles.

Speyside
Between half and two-thirds of Scotland's distilleries, depending
on whose definition you're working with, are situated in the area
around the River Spey and its tributaries in the area between
Aberdeen and Inverness, in the northeast of Scotland.

Islay
Pronounced "Eye-la", this little island off the southwest of
Scotland punches well above its weight, with no fewer than eight
distilleries and a maltings, and another distillery on the way.

The islands
Whisky is produced on several other islands. Mull has
Tobermory Distillery, Arran the Isle of Arran Distillery and
Jura has its namesake distillery. Talisker is situated on Skye
and faraway Orkney is home to two distilleries: Highland
Park and Scapa.

4 Nosing and tasting whisky

A great deal has been written about the right way to taste and nose whisky. The truth of the matter is that, once you've got yourself a decent glass and a decent malt whisky to put in it, you should approach the drink in whatever way makes you happiest. Having said that, however, whisky nosing and tasting becomes more fun, and is considerably easier, if a few ground rules are observed. Just remember to play with them as you see fit.

The lowdown on tasting

The idea of a tumbler of whisky drunk by a roaring fire in a leather armchair under a wall-mounted stag's head is, frankly, out-dated. You can't enjoy whisky properly from a tumbler, particularly in the UK, where a standard measure barely covers the bottom of a glass and is in danger of evaporating before it reaches the lips.

A modern whisky glass has a bulbous bottom to swirl the spirit around and narrows at the top in order to hold in the drink's aromas.

Assessing whisky

We talk about nosing whisky because much of the subtlety of a malt whisky is experienced through the nose, which can discern far more aromas than the tongue can taste flavours. It is important, therefore, to have a glass that will allow you to smell the contents. The ideal malt whisky glass will have a bulbous bottom and a tapered neck, narrowing to the rim so that the aromas are concentrated into a small area at the top. It should also have a base that allows the drinker to hold the glass without cupping the liquid.

Water or no water?

Don't let anyone tell you that you shouldn't add water to malt whisky. In most cases, the malt in your glass has already been mixed with water to bring it down to bottling strength, and, if it has been bottled at cask strength instead, you'll need to add water to bring it down to a tolerable level for drinking.

About four out of five whisky journalists add water to whisky to appreciate it, and blenders and whisky makers will nose spirit diluted to 20% abv. There is a reason for this. Adding water to malt whisky is the equivalent to a spring shower on a rose garden: it's pleasant enough before, but far more fragrant afterwards. Adding water to take malt under 40% isn't for everyone, though.

Take notes

Write down the name of the malt you are tasting, its strength and whether you like it or not. If it reminds you of anything, write that down too, no matter how simplistic or strange it might be. This is your personal record and can take whatever form you like; though, for purposes of comparison, it's advisable to divide your notes into colour, nose, palate and finish.

Appraising

Before you nose or taste a whisky, you can get some valuable clues as to what to expect from it just by appearance. Shake a sample of whisky in a bottle and it will form bubbles on its surface. These disappear again quite quickly. But a whisky with a strong alcoholic content will form small bubbles and they will remain longer. Standard strength, as opposed to cask strength, whiskies will form big bubbles, which will disappear quickly.

Once in the glass, the liquid can be swilled up the side of the glass. Look carefully at traces of whisky on the side of the glass. "Legs" – small columns of liquid – will form and run back down the glass. Slow, thick legs indicate an older whisky.

The biggest clue, though, comes from the colour of the whisky – but it is a clue only. If the whisky has been matured in a bourbon cask, the colour will be more golden lemon and straw-coloured. Sherry casks impart an amber-mahogany colour. Deeper colours may indicate a greater age, but you need to

must know

There are dedicated malt whisky glasses on the market and they're not expensive. But if you have nothing else, a red wine glass or a brandy glass is better than a chunky square tumbler.

Workers at Glenfiddich appraising whisky

By nosing whisky one can gather more information than by tasting.

Colour can be a good indicator of age, for the longer in the cask, the darker the whisky becomes. However, whiskies darken to very different degrees.

be careful with assumptions here. Relatively old whisky from a bourbon cask will be lighter than a much younger sherried whisky, and an older cask that has been used for whisky making before will impart less colour than a first fill cask.

Nosing

Whisky should be approached in the same way that you might approach an unfamiliar animal – slowly and with a great deal of respect. Swirl the whisky around in the glass and then smell it from a distance, gradually bringing it closer to your nose.

This is important because high strength whiskies will have an eye-watering nose prickle and need to be approached with care. Try nosing the whisky with both nostrils at the same time and then one after the other – some people find that one of the three ways of nosing suits them best.

What you're trying to do is identify any familiar smells in the whisky. Can you smell any citrus or berry fruits, is it spicy or smoky, can you smell sherry or vanilla? There are three points to note here. Firstly, don't worry in the least if you can't identify anything in particular at first – it takes a while to get the hang of it. Secondly, whatever you identify is personal to you and there are no rights and wrongs; don't feel intimidated if others seem to be identifying aromas that you just don't get. Thirdly, if you think you smell roast beef and Yorkshire pudding topped with English mustard, write it down and stick with it. As long as it's a smell you would recognise again, it's a suitable descriptor for you.

Adding water often unlocks a whisky and releases its rainbow of aromas, so add a small amount of water if you want to. Take a small taste of the undiluted whisky before you do though.

Tasting

When it comes to tasting, don't sip the whisky but instead put a sizeable amount of it in the mouth and hold it there before swallowing. You can spit it out, but, unless you're going to be tasting a lot of whisky, there's no need to do this.

From the taste you want to try and assess how it feels in the mouth – is it rich and mouth-filling or thin and winey? Is it zesty or fizzy in any way? Does it taste like a whisky, and does it taste nice? Does the taste linger in the mouth when you've swallowed the whisky? The first three questions constitute the "palate", while the fourth refers to the "finish".

Again don't get too hung up on this early on. After all, how do you know a car is fast or slow until you've travelled in a number of vehicles doing a range of speeds? The more whiskies you try, the more reference points you'll have and the easier it'll be. And if that isn't an incentive to keep tasting I don't know what is!

There are several books that go into the subject of nosing and tasting in much more depth, and some people will get immense pleasure out of learning the science of it all and taking it seriously. But you needn't subscribe to that school of thought. Whisky is an organic, evolving, social drink that should be enjoyed. The fun of tasting whisky is just that – tasting it and finding a portfolio of malts that you like and can return to again and again. In essence, it really is as simple as that: do I like the taste of this whisky, and would I want to drink it again?

want to know more?

Classes for learning the skills of nosing and assessing whisky, as well as more informal tasting evenings, can be arranged through many whisky organisations. Here are weblinks to a few recommendations:

• **The Scotch Malt Whisky Society** www.smws.com

• **True Spirit** www.true-spirit.co.uk

• **The following website offers online advice on methods of tasting:** www.scotchwhisky.com

• **Whisky-tasting tours of Scotland can be arranged through** www.scotlandwhisky.com

5 Buying whisky

Entering a specialist whisky shop can be about as appealing as entering a snake pit. On its own, the average old-fashioned whisky bottle is a surly, masculine beast. When gathered together, they come across like a sullen army. It's worse still if they're fronted by a conceited retailer who senses fear the minute the shop door opens. Get to know them, though, and they're a bunch of big softies really. And, these days, many retailers are choosing to discard the funereal outfits; some are even dispensing with the semi-darkness of the specialist retailer and turning up the lights.

Reading the bottle

Bottle labels can be busy places that confuse and confound. The only essential information is the name of the distillery, the age of the whisky, its strength and its price. All else is inessential – although information on the region that the whisky is from may offer a guide to the style, as will tasting notes, if given.

The label for BenRiach Authenticus tells us that it is a single malt (from just one distillery); that the malt has been peated (giving it a distinctly earthy aroma); and that the whisky is at least 21 years old (and so has spent that length of time maturing in oak casks).

Age statements

The age on the bottle of a whisky is a rough guide to its quality, and it will strongly influence what you are going to pay for a bottle. It is only a guide, though, and it doesn't always follow that older means better. The age refers to the youngest whisky in the mix. It is not an average, and nor does it mean that all the whisky is that age – there may be much older whisky in the malt. But if a producer accidentally adds one drop of a younger whisky the whole batch has to be sold at the age of that one drop.

It does happen. A couple of years ago the owners of Ardbeg accidentally added some very young whisky from another of their distilleries to some very old and rare Ardbeg, not only destroying the age but preventing it from being called a single malt any more. But the mix tasted so good that they bottled it under the name Serendipity and sold it without an age on the label.

Which brings us to the next point. If a whisky doesn't have an age statement, it doesn't follow that it is cheap and nasty, or indeed, inferior at all. Johnnie Walker Blue Label, for instance, is one of the most expensive blends on the market, but has no age. This is probably because a small amount of youthful, zesty whisky has been added to the mix to stir up the very special and very rare whiskies it otherwise contains. Under the rules, even a drop of 10-year-old whisky would make the blend a 10-year-old, and would do a disservice to the quality aged whisky that dominates the drink.

Non chill-filtering

Making the perfect malt whisky is a balancing act. As far as possible, the aim is to remove bad tasting flavour compounds but leave in the good ones, and this is the crux of the non chill-filtering debate.

Aberlour a'bunadh is released without an age statement; it is a non chill-filtered whisky and is bottled at cask strength.

When malt whisky is made, a large number of oils and congeners (organic chemicals such as esters, acids and aldehydes) pass into the final liquid. When the liquid is cooled, they naturally solidify and turn the whisky cloudy. This has traditionally been considered unattractive to producers, who want their whisky to be bright and clear. To ensure this, the liquid is chilled until the fats and impurities have solidified, and then the liquid is passed through a filter to remove the solids.

In recent years, however, there has been a lobby of enthusiasts who have argued that the congeners contribute to the full flavour of the malt and that, by removing them, the whisky is left clear but also blander.

A non chill-filtered Ardmore single malt

must know
A non chill-filtered whisky will go cloudy when water is added or if it is cooled. But, argue the purists, it's the real deal and offers the full flavour of whisky.

Macallan Distillery uses ex-sherry oak casks from Spain.

must know

Because of the fact that exchange rates fluctuate so frequently, we have used the local currency, pounds sterling (£), when referring to the cost of specific whiskies. Prices indicated are as accurate as possible at the time of going to press, although increasing competition in the market place means that there are always deals to be had when buying.

In response, some producers have stopped chill-filtering, preferring to sacrifice appearance for taste. Indeed, they have made a virtue of non chill-filtering.

Cask strength

After distillation, the new make spirit will tend to have an alcoholic strength of somewhere in the high 60s% abv (alcohol by volume). Most distilleries put spirit into cask at a strength slightly lower than that, so water is added at the outset. In Scotland, that strength will gradually decline while maturing, but, even after maturation, the cask whisky may still have a strength in the mid or even high 50s% abv.

Most malt whiskies are bottled with a strength of 40%, 43% and occasionally up to 46% abv. To reach these levels, the cask whisky is watered down for bottling. These days, however, it is quite common to find versions of top name whiskies bottled at the strength they came out of the cask. Caution is advised when drinking such whiskies, and even on the nose the acerbic burn of alcohol is pronounced.

It is preferable to add small amounts of chilled water to cask strength whiskies to make them drinkable. The benefit to the drinker is that the added water can release the aromas and flavours of the whisky *(see p40)* but it can still be consumed at full strength. It also means that, effectively, you are getting up to half an extra bottle of whisky for your money. And if ever anyone tells you that you shouldn't add water to malt whisky, point out that, on a standard bottle, someone already has!

Special wood finishes

Although it is not permitted to add anything to the basic mix of barley, water and yeast and call it Scotch whisky (with the exception of caramel for colouring consistency purposes) the rules do allow the whisky to be matured in casks that have contained something else. Indeed, a pre-used cask is essential to the development of Scottish malt.

A common practice among many distillers is to take a whisky out of the oak barrel that it has spent some years in, and finish its maturity in a totally different cask. The time it is in the second cask can be anything from a few weeks to two years or longer. There have been experiments with many types of cask, including rum, Madeira, port, burgundy, Champagne and claret, and there have been a number of "pink" whiskies as a result of the process. The cask also imparts some flavour, usually fruitiness.

This process can enhance malt and produce some excellent results, but don't entirely accept the marketing spiel on the label. The process isn't without its critics, who argue that cask finishing is often used to disguise poor quality malt.

**Balvenie Doublewood
is aged in ex-bourbon barrels,
then finishes its maturation
in ex-sherry casks.**

must know
Cask finishing raises a thorny question. If you're not allowed to add anything to the basic ingredients of malt whisky, how is it possible to add whisky to a substance – namely the wood of the cask – that can substantially affect the taste and colour of the whisky?

Royal Salute The Hundred Cask is a blend limited to just one hundred casks.

Glen Garioch 46-year-old was bottled from whisky distilled in 1958.

Highland Park 30-year-old

Collecting whisky

Buying whisky to collect and store away in a cupboard is akin to buying a stunning painting and putting a blanket over it. A tree grew for 100 years and was then felled, a skilled worker turned it into a cask, a whisky maker made fine malt using a method perfected over generations and filled the cask with it, it sat in a warehouse for a quarter of a century and then some whisky collector sticks it in a cupboard. Sacrilege, bordering on insanity!

However, there are plenty of good reasons to collect whisky as an investment, and even a relatively new aficionado of the whisky world will learn how to spot potential whisky cash cows.

Old whisky

This refers to two different things: whisky that dates from many years ago, and whisky that might have gone into the bottle relatively recently but was in the cask for a long time. In the first case, old whisky will have a value because, as time goes by, whiskies get rarer as people drink them. Hence their value to collectors. In the second case, the older a whisky gets in the cask, the less there is of it, because some will have evaporated – the "angels' share". The older the whisky, then, the rarer it is.

The Glenrothes Distillers Edition 1975

Limited bottlings
From time to time distilleries bottle the product of just one or two specific casks, limiting it to a very small number of bottles. A decidedly old whisky cask might only produce in the region of 120 bottles, and, of course, that makes it rare and sought after. Bottlings for special occasions, such as to mark a special anniversary or national event, will also tend to have a collectible value.

Big name distilleries
Some distilleries have a loyal and passionate following, and special or rare bottlings from them have extra value to the collector because they are more greatly sought after. Islay and iconic island malts fall into this bracket, as do some of the best-known Speyside malts.

Closed distilleries
Once a distillery is closed down it can, of course, no longer make whisky, and therefore, as stocks are depleted or run out entirely, existing bottles become collectors' items. Some distilleries have taken on an almost mythical status since they shut. A bottle of Rosebank or Port Ellen, for example, would always be a good investment.

want to know more?
For whisky advice and recommendations, Whisky Magazine (www.whiskymag.com) regularly rounds up current releases. The equivalent publication in the USA is The Malt Advocate (www.malt advocate.com).

The UK's best whisky outlets include:
• The Whisky Shop, which has 13 outlets across Britain (www.whiskyshop.com)
• The Whisky Exchange – Britain's most comprehesive retailer (www.thewhisky exchange.com)
• Loch Fyne Whiskies – a great independent retailer (www.lfw.co.uk)

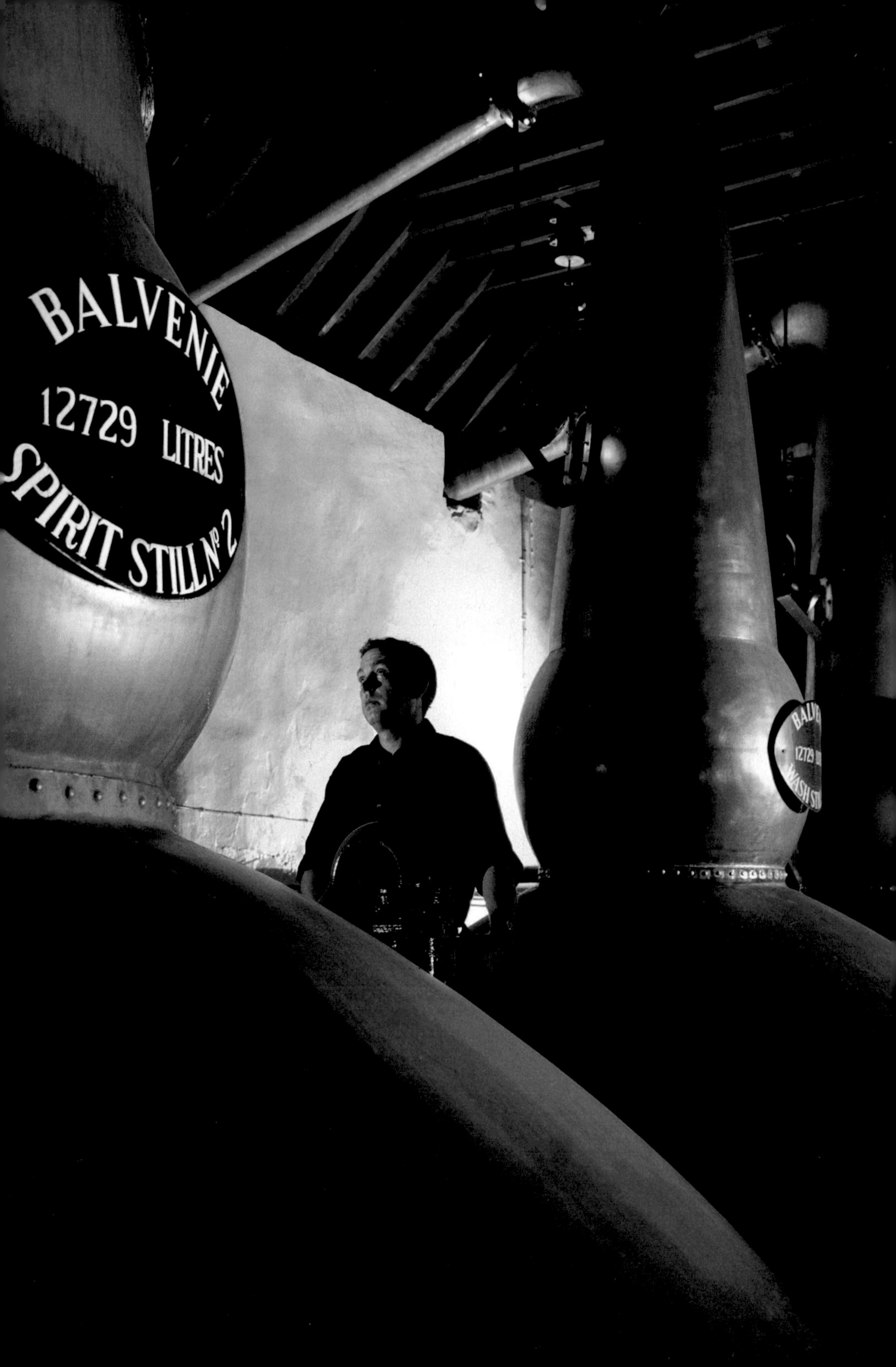
BALVENIE
12729 LITRES
SPIRIT STILL Nº 2

6 Scotland's distilleries

Scotland's distilleries form an organic mass, constantly shifting and changing as they open and close with the whims of the whisky economy. At the moment, we're in a boom period for single malts, as drinkers seek out products with provenance. A trend has developed for drinking less whisky but of better quality, and the increased worldwide demand for the spirit – from France to South America, as well as the emerging markets in Southeast Asia and Russia – has a considerable bearing on the distilleries of Scotland.

Scotland's distilleries

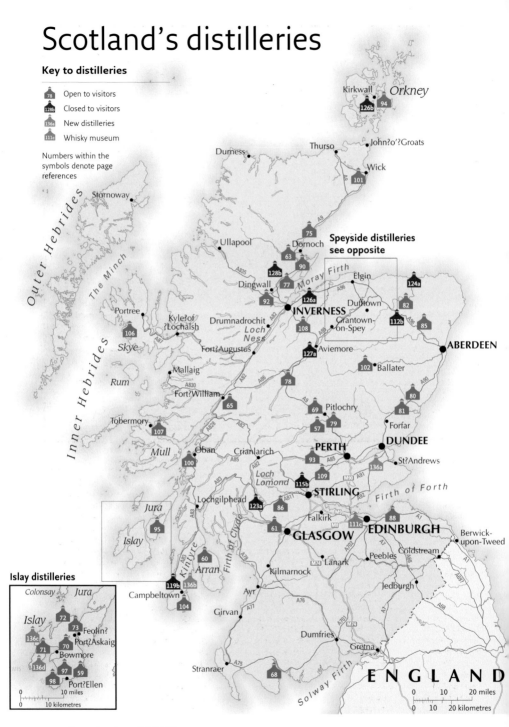

Key to distilleries

- [78] Open to visitors
- [128b] Closed to visitors
- [136a] New distilleries
- [111c] Whisky museum

Numbers within the symbols denote page references

Orkney

Kirkwall [126b] [94]

Thurso John?o'?Groats

Wick

[101]

Durness

Stornoway

Outer Hebrides

The Minch

Ullapool

[75]
Dornoch
[63]
[90]

Speyside distilleries see opposite

[128b]
Dingwall [77]
Elgin [124a]
[92]
[126a]
Moray Firth
INVERNESS
Dufftown [82]
[112b] [85]

Portree
[106]
Kyle?of?Lochalsh
Drumnadrochit
Loch Ness
Grantown-on-Spey
ABERDEEN

Skye

Inner Hebrides

Fort?Augustus
[108]
[127a]
Aviemore

[102] Ballater

Rum

Mallaig

Fort?William
[65]
[78]

[80]
[69] Pitlochry
[81]
[57] [79]
Forfar

Tobermory
[107]

Mull

Oban
[100]
Crianlarich
PERTH
[93]
DUNDEE
St?Andrews

Loch Lomond
[109]
[136a]

[115b]
STIRLING
Firth of Forth

Jura
[95]

Lochgilphead
[123a] [86]
Falkirk
[88]
[61]
[111c]
GLASGOW
EDINBURGH

Islay

Berwick-upon-Tweed

Kintyre
[60]
Arran

Firth of Clyde

Kilmarnock
Lanark
Peebles
Coldstream

[119b] [136b]
Campbeltown
[104]

Ayr
Jedburgh

Girvan

Dumfries
Gretna

Stranraer
[68]

E N G L A N D

Solway Firth

Islay distilleries

Colonsay Jura

Islay
[72]

[73] Feolin?
[136c]
Port?Askaig
[71] [70]
Bowmore
[136d]
[97] [59]
[98]
Port?Ellen

0   10 miles
0   10 kilometres

0   10   20 miles
0   10   20 kilometres

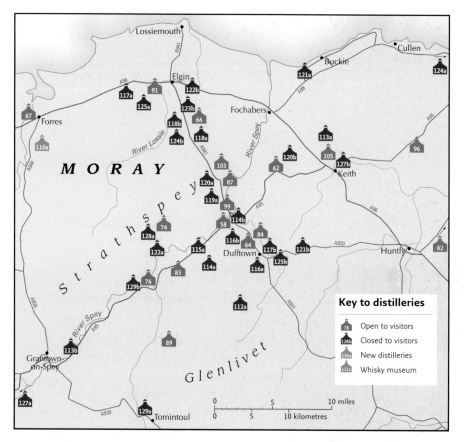

Key to distilleries

🏭 78   Open to visitors
🏭 128b   Closed to visitors
🏭 136a   New distilleries
🏭 111c   Whisky museum

0   5   10 miles
0   5   10 kilometres

Open to visitors

Aberfeldy 57	Dalwhinnie 78	Macallan 99
Aberlour 58	Edradour 79	Oban 100
Ardbeg 59	Fettercairn 80	Pulteney 101
Arran 60	Glencadam 81	Royal Lochnagar 102
Auchentoshan 61	Glendronach 82	Speyburn 103
Auchroisk 62	Glenfarclas 83	Springbank 104
Balblair 63	Glenfiddich 84	Strathisla 105
Balvenie 64	Glen Garioch 85	Talisker 106
Ben Nevis 65	Glengoyne 86	Tobermory 107
Benriach 66	Glen Grant 87	Tomatin 108
Benromach 67	Glenkinchie 88	Tullibardine 109
Bladnoch 68	Glenlivet 89	
Blair Athol 69	Glenmorangie 90	**Whisky museums**
Bowmore 70	Glen Moray 91	Dallas Dhu 110a
Bruichladdich 71	Glen Ord 92	Scotch Whisky Heritage
Bunnahabhain 72	Glenturret 93	Centre 111c
Caol Ila 73	Highland Park 94	
Cardhu 74	Jura 95	
Clynelish 75	Knockdhu 96	
Cragganmore 76	Lagavulin 97	
Dalmore 77	Laphroaig 98	

Closed to visitors

Allt-a-Bhainne 112a	Linkwood 122b
Ardmore 112b	Loch Lomond 123a
Aultmore 113a	Longmorn 123b
Balmenach 113b	Macduff 124a
Benrinnes 114a	Mannochmore 124b
Craigellachie 114b	Miltonduff 125a
Dailuaine 115a	Mortlach 125b
Deanston 115b	Royal Brackla 126a
Dufftown 116a	Scapa 126b
Glenallachie 116b	Speyside 127a
Glenburgie 117a	Strathmill 127b
Glendullan 117b	Tamdhu 128a
Glen Elgin 118a	Teaninch 128b
Glenlossie 118b	Tomintoul 129a
Glenrothes 119a	Tormore 129b
Glen Scotia 119b	
Glen Spey 120a	**New distilleries**
Glentauchers 120b	Daftmill 136a
Inchgower 121a	Glengyle 136b
Kininvie 121b	Kilchoman 136c
Knockando 122a	Port Charlotte 136d

The distillery listings

The following distillery guide is designed to give you some contextual information about bottles of malt whisky you may have come across, to help you understand the whisky better and to provide pointers about distilleries to take your interest further.

The cooperage at Balvenie

About the listings

There are two main sections to the chapter and, in each, distilleries are listed alphabetically. The first section *(pp57–109)* lists distilleries that you can visit; they either have visitor centres or offer tours. The second section *(pp112–29)* lists distilleries that produce malts but do not generally allow visitors.

Following the two main sections is a short round-up *(pp130–34)* of closed distilleries whose whiskies are, nevertheless, still available. There is then a final "oddball" section *(pp135–37)*, which includes distilleries you might come across but that don't fit into any of the other categories. These include strange bottlings that are hard to pin down, distilleries elsewhere in the UK and some new distilleries to look out for in Scotland.

Core ranges and signature expressions

In these listings, you will see by the side of each entry, a short list of the core bottlings from each distillery, along with a signature expression that is singled out to best represent the distillery.

Some entries also highlight a special bottle with which to treat yourself – one that you might choose for a special occasion or if unconcerned by the cost.

Aberfeldy

Region: Highlands

Set in wonderful surroundings, easy to reach and offering two distinct visitor experiences, Aberfeldy and the Dewar's World of Whisky exhibition make for an impressive package.

The distillery

A tour of the pretty distillery itself is worthwhile for the more serious whisky enthusiast. It offers an overview of the malt whisky production, while Dewar's World of Whisky focuses on the Dewar's blend. The Aberfeldy malt is very much underrated. It's a rich, honeyed and oily whisky, with full flavours, particularly in the 21-year-old.

Visiting details

Launched at the start of the millennium, Dewar's World of Whisky concentrates on Dewar's blended whisky, which has the Aberfeldy malt at its heart. The exhibition includes a recreation of a 19th-century blending room – with the addition of interactive displays – and Tommy Dewar's library at his London-based headquarters. Posters and other advertising material demonstrate the potency and imagination of the Dewar's company as it developed into an internationally recognised brand. *See also p110.*

must know

Contact details
Aberfeldy, Perthshire
01887 822010

www.aberfeldy.com
www.dewarsworldofwhisky.com

Core range
Aberfeldy 12-year-old
Aberfeldy 21-year-old

Signature malt
Aberfeldy 12-year-old:
rich, oily and fresh, with a zesty tangerine note.

Dewar's World of Whisky at Aberfeldy

Aberlour

Region: Speyside

Size-wise Aberlour is just about perfect, and, nestled at the end of the town's busy main street, it remains largely as it was when completed by architect Charles Doig at the end of the 19th century.

The distillery

Aberlour is one of those pretty and unforgettable distilleries, with a relatively new visitor facility. The tour, conducted by knowledgeable staff, is unhurried and thorough, while the whisky has a rich, satisfying taste, and is particularly cherished in France.

Visiting details

Aberlour has taken a pioneering approach to distillery tours, offering an in-depth experience designed to please even the most demanding of enthusiasts. Lasting an hour and 45 minutes, the tour includes a chance to sample the wort and the wash, and ends with a lengthy and relaxed tasting session of the final whisky.

Aberlour
a'bunadh

   To cap it off you are presented with a stylish 50-page booklet and given the opportunity to pay extra to fill a bottle of Aberlour for yourself from either a sherry or a bourbon cask. If you decide to do this, go for the bourbon cask – it gives an unusual take on a respected whisky and reveals another layer of flavours in the malt.

Aberlour Distillery

Ardbeg

Region: Islay

Ardbeg is one of the "big three" distilleries that sit next to each other in what might be called whisky nirvana. South Islay's whiskies are famous for their distinctive peaty, smoky style.

The distillery

The sea laps across the rocky shoreline right up to the distillery walls, and arguably there are few experiences finer than drinking malt here, straight from the cask on a blustery and sunny Islay day. If peaty, tangy, tarry and oily whisky is your thing, the offering here is sublime. In addition to the core range, cask strength bottlings and a few oddballs are also on offer – if you can still get them. Very Young, Still Young and Almost There are separate bottlings that track the maturation of the signature 10-year-old from six years up to full maturity. There are also some fantastic special bottlings originally casked before 1980. Be warned though: Ardbeg can easily become a very expensive lifelong pursuit.

Visiting details

The word "quaint" might have been invented for Ardbeg, and a ramshackle tour here takes you past hand-painted signs and a medley of traditional distilling equipment. It ends in what used to be the kiln for malting barley and is now one of the finest cafés in Scotland, with homemade meals and afternoon treats ensuring that even the unconverted whisky enthusiasts in your party are left satisfied.

must know

Contact details
Port Ellen, Isle of Islay
01496 302244

www.ardbeg.com

Core range
Ardbeg 10-year-old
Ardbeg 17-year-old
Kildalton
Provenance 1974
Uigeadail
Airigh Nam Beist
Lord of the Isles

Signature malt
Ardbeg 10-year-old:
a meal in a glass; cocoa, oily fish, swirling peat and chewy sweetness married together perfectly. Truly exceptional.

Arran

Region: Islands

Arran was recently chosen by *Whisky Magazine* as its "Distillery of the Year", which is an amazing achievement for a whisky producer that has only been operating for just over 10 years.

The distillery

Since it started producing whisky, Arran has had something of a scattergun approach to releasing malts, and in the early days released some ropey young whiskies. But there was a dramatic transformation when the whisky reached seven years old, and by the time the distillery was bottling a 10-year-old it had turned into a glorious swan of a malt. Its rich creaminess is credited to its location at Lochranza, where it sits in a suntrap in the Gulf Stream and benefits from a benign climate. Recent cask strength and non chill-filtered versions of the malt are particularly impressive. Also keep an eye out for one of the occasional special cask finishes.

Visiting details

The visitor centre includes a shop and restaurant, and tours include an audio-visual presentation held in a mock-up of an old crofter's cottage. The distillery tour follows a logical route and is ideal for beginners. The guides here are great too. The distillery has reduced opening hours in winter and is shut in January and February.

must know

Contact details
Lochranza, Isle of Arran
01786 431900

www.arranwhisky.com

Core range
Arran 10-year-old
The Arran Malt
Arran 100 proof
Robert Burns Single Malt
Cask bottlings

Signature malt
Arran 10-year-old:
creamy, rich mix of citrus, toffee and butterscotch. Very chewy and quite delightful.

The clean-cut Arran Distillery

Auchentoshan

Region: Lowland

Auchentoshan sits on the outskirts of Glasgow and its whisky is special because it is a triple distilled single malt. The distillery offers a friendly and informal visiting experience.

The distillery

Auchentoshan bears the trademark characteristics of a Lowland malt in that it is a light, easy-to-drink malt. But owner Morrison Bowmore has put a great deal of effort into offering a range of different expressions of Auchentoshan, and some of the more recent bottlings show a surprising and impressive diversity. It's worth comparing the clean, subtle and citrusy 18-year-old alongside the Three Wood, for example – the latter drenched in distinctive sherry flavours. If this is your kind of whisky, look out for the Auchentoshan Limited Editions, which are fantastic examples of the very best Auchentoshan casks.

Visiting details

The tour takes in the full production process, including an attractive still room and a visit to the warehouse. Should you wish to, you can fill your own bottle at the end of the tour and put a personalised label on it. VIP tours are also available, as is the distillery manager's masterclass, for more serious enthusiasts. Both should be booked in advance. Auchentoshan is open seven days a week, except over Christmas and New Year. It is all on one level, and so is ideal for wheelchair users.

must know

Contact details
Clydebank, Glasgow
01389 878561

www.auchentoshan.com

Core range
Auchentoshan Select,
Auchentoshan 10-year-old,
Auchentoshan Three Wood
Auchentoshan 21-year-old

Signature malt
Auchentoshan 10-year-old:
light and smooth, with a hint of citrus; very accessible to the beginner.

Auchroisk

Region: Speyside

Producing 3.1 million litres, Auchroisk is a relatively modern distillery, built in 1974 to supply what was then the International Distiller and Vintner group (IDV) with malt for blending.

The distillery

The choice of location was taken after careful consideration and so, perhaps unsurprisingly, the distillery's malt proved to be of high quality. At least some of it has been bottled as a single malt since the mid-1980s. Early bottlings were known as The Singleton, but the distillery's name is now used.

Visiting details

Although the distillery is a modern one, having been built only 35 years ago, it hasn't got any dedicated visitor facilities as such. However, it is open to the public all year round, Mondays to Fridays, and staff will conduct tours by prior arrangement.

must know

Contact details
Ulben, Banffshire
01542 885000

www.malts.com

Core range
Auchroisk 10-year-old
Auchroisk 28-year-old Rare Malt

Signature malt
Auchroisk 10

Go on, treat yourself ...
Auchroisk 28-year-old RareMalt

Balblair

Region: Highlands

Situated close to the high profile Glenmorangie Distillery, Balblair is rather modest and unassuming by comparison – somewhat surprising, given that its name means "battlefield".

The distillery

In recent years, Balblair has worked to reposition the distillery's malts to focus on vintage bottlings rather than the standard age expressions. That, along with some very impressive premium packaging, suggests Balblair is a malt that's going places. They say that the air around the distillery is the purest in Scotland and Balblair associates itself with this purity. But Balblair isn't a lightweight, and has some distinctive earthy and spicy flavours that make it an attractive and satisfying malt.

Visiting details

Although there are no visitor facilities, tours can be arranged by appointment. Visitors are shown around the distillery and the traditional dunnage warehouses, and are offered a whisky in the old maltings room. This highly personalised tour is conducted by the distillery manager or the assistant distillery manager.

Balblair Vintage 1979

must know

Contact details
Edderton, Ross-Shire
01862 821273

www.inverhouse.com

Core range
Vintage 1997
Vintage 1989
Vintage 1979

Signature malt
Vintage 1997:
this is classic Balblair –
full-bodied, clean, rich and
fruity. In the older vintages,
flavours include apricot,
orange, green apple, cloves,
vanilla and honey.

Balvenie

Region: Speyside

Balvenie is the sister distillery to Glenfiddich, the world's biggest malt distillery. What it lacks in scale and quantity, Balvenie more than makes up for in quality, with its fruity, honeyed whiskies.

The distillery

Balvenie is situated on the same site as Glenfiddich and owner William Grant's third distillery, Kininvie. Balvenie's output is very much a whisky lover's whisky, its distinctive toffeeness earning it a reputation as one of Speyside's top whiskies. It is the perfect foil to the glitzy Glenfiddich: a traditional craft distillery that does things the old-fashioned way.

Visiting details

A special pre-booked tour lasting two and a half hours and restricted to just eight people gives visitors the chance to see a traditional distillery up close and personal. The tour includes a look at one of the few remaining floor maltings in existence and ends with a tasting session in the old distillery manager's cottage. All in all, it is sufficiently in-depth to keep even the most inquisitive whisky enthusiast happy.

must know

Contact details
Dufftown, Banffshire
01340 820373

www.thebalvenie.com

Core range
Founders Reserve 10-year-old
Doublewood 12-year-old
Single Barrel 15-year-old
Port Wood 21-year-old

Signature malt
Doublewood 12-year-old:
chewy rich fruits and the most
exquisite Speyside honey.

Go on, treat yourself...
The 21-year-old is quite possible
the best example there is of a
whisky finished in port pipes, but
the 30-year-old is a world-class
big hitter, dressed in ermine.

**Balvenie
Doublewood**

Ben Nevis

Region: Highlands

Ben Nevis Distillery sits beneath the mountain of the same name on Scotland's west coast, and while it isn't the prettiest of distilleries, it is one of Scotland's most visited.

The distillery

The stunning location and a sympathetic refurbishment by its Japanese owners draw visitors to Ben Nevis. The distillery has had a chequered past, but is now approaching its 20th anniversary since the acquisition by Japan's second largest distiller, Nikka, and a steady flow of quality 10-year-old and the occasional special bottling have established it as a solid malt producer. Ben Nevis is one of the very few distilleries that bottles a single malt and a blend under the same name, so check what you're buying. The distillery also sells its own Glencoe blend, which is eight years old.

Visiting details

Distillery tours incur a small charge here. However, the tour does include a whisky taster, and the full admission price is redeemable against the purchase of a bottle in the shop, should you wish. The distillery is open all year round, though there are reduced hours in winter and only weekend visits by prior arrangement between October and Easter.

BenRiach

Region: Speyside

BenRiach is one of the most exciting distilleries currently operating in Scotland. In recent years, variety has become its raison d'être, and barely a month goes by without a new whisky.

The distillery

After a chequered history, BenRiach was taken on by a consortium headed by Billy Walker in 2004, since when it has gone into whisky overdrive. At a time when conventional logic dictates that distilleries should offer a small and simple range of whiskies, we're getting all sorts of curveballs from Billy and his team; fortunately, most of them are excellent.

If you're in the mood to treat yourself, try the Authenticus. Aged for 21 years, this is a growling beast of a peated whisky, less sweet than an Islay malt and nicely rounded by the years in the cask.

Visiting details

The distillery itself is small but easy to find and has perfectly-preserved floor maltings. Although the distillery doesn't have a visitor centre and doesn't advertise tours, the owners say that they like to think of the whole site as a visitor experience and staff are only too happy to show people around if they book in advance.

must know

Contact details
Longmorn, near Elgin,
Morayshire
01343 862888

www.benriachdistillery.co.uk

Core range
Heart of Speyside 12, 16,
and 20-year-olds
Curiositas
Authenticus
Hereditus Fumosus
Authenticus Fumosus
Arumaticus Fumosus
Benriach 15-year-old in a range
of wood finishes

Signature malt
Heart of Speyside 12-year-old:
as Speyside as Speyside gets –
all rich fruit and honey, held in
place by a balanced oak and
malt lining. Delightful.

The old BenRiach barrel train for tranferring casks

Benromach

Region: Speyside

The smallest distillery in Speyside, Benromach is operated by just two men. Since independent bottlers Gordon & MacPhail took it on, the distillery has enjoyed its healthiest period.

The distillery

When Gordon & MacPhail bought Benromach, some 15 years ago, it had fallen on hard times, and a raggle-taggle assortment of equipment was brought in from elsewhere to get it back up and running. Gordon & MacPhail know the mysteries of wood management as well as anyone else in the industry, so it should come as no surprise to learn that the distillery is starting to produce some excellent wood finished malts. Benromach has also launched an organic whisky. To achieve organic recognition, the casks have had to be made with organic oak – in this case new American oak. New oak impacts heavily on the spirit, and there is a distinctive orange liqueur characteristic to the whisky – which is delicious.

Visiting details

This cosy distillery is open all year round apart from 10 days over Christmas, with reduced hours in winter. The small tour charge is redeemable against the cost of a bottle of whisky in the shop. Visitors also have the opportunity to fill a bottle of Benromach for themselves.

Benromach Traditional

must know

Contact details
Forres, Moray
01309 675968

www.benromach.com

Core range
Benromach Traditional
Benromach Organic
Benromach Peat Smoke
Tokaji
Sassicaia
Portwood
Benromach 25-year-old

Signature malt
Benromach Traditional:
a delicate mix of malt and fruit with a spicy afterglow and a trace of smoke.

Go on, treat yourself...
Benromach 21-year-old:
a heady mix of sherry, dark fruits, oak and spice. Exquisite.

Bladnoch

Region: Lowlands

Bladnoch enjoys a cult status among some whisky enthusiasts, having been brought back from the brink by an Irishman who initially set out to turn the mothballed distillery into holiday homes.

The distillery

Bladnoch's brush with mortality was laid to rest when the Irishman in question himself joined the campaign to re-establish the distillery. It is a very small and isolated distillery, and produces a style of whisky that for a long time was deeply neglected – the light, floral, Lowland type.

The new owner, Raymond Armstrong, has released some of the older stock in recent years, but all eyes are on what happens next. Those that have tasted the new spirit say that it is in keeping with the region, and very "flowery".

Visiting details

About 25,000 visitors make their way to Bladnoch each year and few of them leave disappointed. It is a pretty, small distillery, and offers tours and tastings. Intermittently, it also opens up a special whisky school, in which pupils can start work early on Friday morning and take part in distillery production and training – "graduating" two and a half days later.

---

must know

Contact details
Wigtown, Wigtownshire
01988 402605

www.bladnoch.co.uk

Core range
Bladnoch 10-year-old
Bladnoch 12-year-old
Bladnoch 13-year-old
Bladnoch 15-year-old

Signature malt
Bladnoch 10-year-old:
almost defines the Lowland style, with floral and light citrus notes and a complex mix of other influences.

Go on, treat yourself...
Bladnoch 15-year-old:
the cask strength is chewier, more intense and with more depth than the normal bottlings.

Blair Athol

Region: Highlands

Blair Athol lies close to the A9, not far from Edradour Distillery, in the region of the Highlands to the south of Speyside. Consequently, it is easy to reach from Scotland's main cities.

The distillery

Blair Athol is a sizeable distillery, capable of producing about two million litres a year. But very little of this is bottled as a single malt, and it has just one core expression, the Blair Athol 12-year-old. The vast majority of its malt output goes into the heart of Bell's blended whisky.

The distillery itself is one of the oldest working distilleries in Scotland, having been established in 1798, a whole century before many others close to it.

Visiting details

Blair Athol is open daily from June to October, and offers a limited number of tours and reduced opening times at other times of the year. As with most Diageo distilleries, a charge is levied, but one that is redeemable against a 70cl bottle purchase. Children under eight are welcome but not permitted in the production areas.

must know

Contact details
Pitlochry, Perthshire
01796 482003

www.discovering-distilleries.com

Signature malt
Blair Athol 12-year-old:
unfussy and richly fruity.

Go on, treat yourself ...
A very rare 27-year-old would definitely be worth investigation – if you can find a bottle.

Most of Blair Athol's output goes into Bell's blended whisky.

Bowmore

Region: Islay

Bowmore is in the middle of Islay, and in terms of peating levels, its whiskies are in the central ground too, with the distinctive Islay taste but without the phenol and fish peaks of some Islay whiskies.

The distillery

In the past, Bowmore suffered from producing too many different styles of whisky, so the owners are now focusing on a smaller core range. It's a beautiful whisky, with a distinctive "parma violet" note on some expressions. Bowmore is a wonderful place to visit too. It improved its facilities a couple of years ago and now has a visitor centre that boasts stunning views across Loch Indaal to Bruichladdich Distillery. When the breeze is up and the sun flits across the busy waves that lap up to the distillery, take a glass of Bowmore and drink it whilst sitting on the sea wall – you'll never feel more alive!

Bowmore also has its own floor maltings and huge peat-burning fires, so you can see and smell the work in progress.

Visiting details

Bowmore is open all year round: every day from July to mid-September; and Monday to Saturday the rest of the year. The tour includes a visit to the famous No. 1 vault, and concludes with a dram overlooking Loch Indaal.

must know

Contact details
Bowmore, Isle of Islay
01496 810441

www.bowmore.com

Core range
Bowmore 12-year-old
Bowmore 15-year-old "Darkest"
Bowmore 18-year-old
Bowmore 25-year-old

Signature malt
Bowmore 12-year-old:
the classic Bowmore, with a lovely balance of oak, malt, sea notes and mid-range peat smoke.

Go on treat yourself...
Bowmore 18-year-old:
this is a delight. The balance of floating smoke, fruit and oak wrap around the distinctive and chunky malt perfectly.

Bowmore 25-year-old

Bruichladdich

Region: Islay

Bruichladdich reopened its doors some seven years ago when it was bought by independent bottler Murray McDavid. It is the last independently owned distillery on Islay.

The distillery

Bruichladdich is fiercely proud of its independence and tends to play the role of maverick, portraying itself as a people's champion – a (Murray Mc)David against the industry goliaths. But with the highly-respected Jim McEwan in charge of production and a swashbuckling approach to whisky making that has seen it create all sorts of eyebrow-raising concoctions, there's rarely been a dull moment at the distillery. A knowledge of all the bottlings over the last few years would make a great subject for an appearance on Mastermind. Bruichladdich has great packaging too.

Visiting details

Tours can take place throughout the year, but you are advised to ring in advance to book. There is a small charge, but the price includes a dram of whisky, and tours last for about 45 minutes. The distillery also has a shop.

must know

Contact details
Bruichladdich, Isle of Islay
01496 850221

www.bruichladdich.com

Core range
Bruichladdich 10-year-old
Bruichladdich 12-year-old
Bruichladdich 15-year-old
Bruichladdich XVII

Signature malt
Bruichladdich 10-year-old:
clean, unpeaty, sweet and
fruity; very more-ish.

Go on, treat yourself ...
Bruichladdich XVII:
Very fresh – almost zesty –
and on its best behaviour,
but with enough bite to
keep you interested.

Bunnahabhain

Region: Islay

Bunnahabhain has been enjoying a resurgence recently, by turning the traditional disadvantage of being an unpeated whisky from the "peat capital" island of Islay into a positive selling point.

The whisky

Pronounced "Boo-na-ha-venn", Bunnahabhain is now in the ownership of Burn Stewart, who has been promoting the whisky as the "gentle taste of Islay". It has developed a growing following of loyalists, and Burn Stewart has now launched an impressive 18-year-old and 25-year-old to sit alongside the delightful 12-year-old. At last the distillery is starting to enjoy its place in the sun.

Visiting details

Bunnahabhain is a gem of a distillery, and well worth seeking out. It enjoys an idyllic location overlooking the seething waters of the Sound of Jura and has a view across to the famous Paps of Jura. It is a small, intimate and very friendly place, and there is nothing rushed about the tour here.

From the end of April until mid-October there are three tours a day from Monday to Thursday. At other times, personal tours with the distillery manager can be arranged by appointment.

must know

Contact details
Port Askaig, Isle of Islay
01496 840646

www.bunnahabhain.com

Core range
Bunnahabhain 12-year-old
Bunnahabhain 18-year-old
Bunnahabhain 25-year-old

Signature malt
Bunnahabhain 12-year-old:
a rare unpeated Islay whisky but very much a maritime one, with sharp fruit and salty tang giving it its personality.

Go on, treat yourself...
Bunnahabhain 25-year-old:
released in late 2005, this is a weighty whisky, with rich plum and sherry notes. The wood does just enough to make this a truly memorable drinking experience.

Bunnahabhain
Distillery

Caol Ila

Region: Islay

Situated near the harbour at Port Askaig, Caol Ila is the biggest whisky producer on Islay. It's not the best known, however, as most of its malt goes into blends, particularly Johnnie Walker's.

The distillery

Caol Ila is not the prettiest distillery on Islay or the most famous, but nevertheless its profile has been raised substantially in recent years. In 2001, partially because of stock problems with Diageo's other peated Islay whisky Lagavulin, Caol Ila started to be sold as a single malt in three different expressions. It has since become the island's fastest growing malt – which is no wonder, as this is a truly special whisky, and the 18-year-old, in particular, is up there with the very best.

The distillery might not be the prettiest, but the location is, and Caol Ila shares Bunnahabhain's view across the bubbling water to the Paps of Jura.

Visiting details

The distillery is open to the public for tours if they are booked in advance. They take place Monday to Friday throughout the year, though hours are restricted in winter. There is a small charge that's redeemable against a purchase in the distillery shop. Children under eight are not permitted in the production areas.

must know

Contact details
Port Askaig, Islay
01496 302760

www.malts.com

Core range
Caol Ila 12-year-old
Caol Ila 18-year-old
Caol Ila Cask strength
Caol Ila 25-year-old

Signature malt
Caol Ila 12-year-old:
oily, with a seaside barbecue combination of smoky bacon and grilled sardines.

Go on, treat yourself...
The 25-year-old:
age has given this whisky citrusy notes among the oil and sea notes – as if someone has squeezed a lemon over a sunflower oil-soaked sardine, cooking over charcoal.

Caol Ila 12-year-old

Cardhu

Region: Speyside

Cardhu is the symbolic home of Johnnie Walker, and its malt is a main component in the range of Walker blends. But, for all its high-profile associations, Cardhu exists in a whisky limbo-land.

The distillery

A funny old malt, Cardhu. It enjoys a huge market in Southern Europe, particularly in Spain, and is much in demand for blending. In certain circles, it is even regarded as malt at its very finest. Yet it receives none of the acclaim in its homeland that's usually reserved for great Speysiders; it attracts a relatively small number of visitors too. More's the pity really, as it is a charming distillery, with a colourful and important history. In the 1870s, for example, it was run by Elizabeth Cumming, then known to all as "the Queen of the Whisky Trade".

must know

Contact details
Aberlour, Banffshire
01340 872555

www.malts.com

Signature malt
Cardhu 12-year-old:
sweet, very malty, very clean
and very drinkable.

Visiting details

Cardhu is the home of Johnnie Walker, but Cardhu doesn't make as much of the link as, say, Dewar's does at Aberfeldy, or The Famous Grouse at Glenturret. It's a lovely distillery to visit, and the small charge for admission is redeemable against a 70cl bottle purchased at the shop. The distillery is open all year round, with reduced hours in winter.

**Cardhu
12-year-old**

Clynelish

Region: Highlands

Clynelish is rather enigmatic. It is both a seaside malt and a Highland one, and it contains characteristics of both. This is far from where the confusion ends, however...

The distillery

To complicate matters further, Clynelish is situated in the town of Brora, next to another distillery which was originally called Clynelish but changed its name to Brora. For a short time, the two distilleries operated side by side as Clynelish 1 and 2, before the older one shut its doors for good and the second became what is now called Clynelish.

The distillery produces a big, rich, stylish and smoky malt, and is very much recommended. But it's nowhere near as peaty as the original Clynelish style and the other whiskies produced at Brora. The Brora 30-year-old is almost as perfect as whisky gets (see p132). Fans of today's Clynelish, however, point to its salty flavour and overall assertiveness.

(see p132)

Visiting details

Clynelish is in a stunning, if a little remote, location. It welcomes visitors throughout the year, although from November to Easter you'll need to make an appointment first. There is a modest fee, but the tour includes a free dram and the entrance price is redeemable against the purchase of a bottle. Children are welcome but cannot be admitted to the production areas if they are under eight.

must know

Contact details
Brora, Sutherland
01408 623000

www.malts.com

Signature malt
Clynelish 14-year-old: whisky's equivalent to Nascar: smoke, oil, and a big engine.

Clynelish Distillery

Cragganmore

Region: Speyside

Built during a boom time for whisky in 1869, Cragganmore was sited by the River Spey. More importantly, however, it had access to the railway, a vital freight link to the blenders down south.

The whisky

Cragganmore was chosen a few years back as one of Diageo's six "classic malts", it representing the Speyside region in that collection. Yet it is something of an oddball, and probably isn't the first whisky that would spring to mind if you were to draw up a list of classic Speyside malts. In fact, you perhaps wouldn't think of Diageo at all in this regard, even though it owns a fair few Speyside distilleries, including those producing such elegant whiskies as Glen Elgin and Linkwood. Nevertheless, Cragganmore is a sophisticated sweet-and-sour fruit mix of a whisky, produced by one of the company's smallest distilleries.

Visiting details

The distillery allows a limited number of tours from May until October, but places need to be booked in advance. There is a small visitor centre that was reopened two years ago.

must know

Contact details
Ballindalloch, Banffshire
01340 872555

www.discovering-distilleries.com

Core range
Cragganmore 12-year-old
Distiller's Edition Double Matured

Signature malt
Cragganmore 12-year-old:
complex and rich Speyside
fruit with a much less typically
Speyside tangy undertow.

Go on, treat yourself...
Cragganmore 17-year-old:
Bottled at cask strength
and limited to a few
thousand bottles.

**Cragganmore
Distillery**

Dalmore

Region: Highlands

Dalmore Distillery lies amidst stunning scenery on the East Highland coastal road. It takes some getting to, but this is a wonderful part of the world, and the whisky is worth the trek.

The distillery

In the last 10 years, The Dalmore has started to not only earn the plaudits it deserves, but also to win over whisky drinkers. However, some believe it can achieve much, much more, and, in terms of quality, is up there with Dalwhinnie and Clynelish as one of the very best Highland distilleries. The whisky has hit the headlines in recent years because one or two of its very oldest whiskies – more than 60 years old – have fetched tens of thousands of pounds at auction. You really don't have to spend that, though, and who wouldn't readily swap one veteran bottle for a lifetime's supply of the 12-year-old?

Visiting details

Dalmore's visitor centre is open from Monday to Friday and offers tours. Weekend appointments can be made, but you are advised to book in advance. There is a small charge for tours and children under eight are not permitted in the production area.

Dalmore
12-year-old

must know

Contact details
Alness, Ross-shire
01349 882362

www.thedalmore.com

Core range
The Dalmore 12-year-old
The Dalmore 21-year-old
The Cigar Malt

Signature malt
The Dalmore 12-year-old:
muscular and quite stunning
Highland malt, with orange
notes and a solid oak and
malt platform.

Go on, treat yourself...
The Dalmore 21-year-old:
lush, orange, grapefruit and
stewed fruits, all enriched by
the ageing wood. Truly great.

Dalwhinnie

Region: Highlands

Dalwhinnie sits in one of the coldest spots in the UK, and its supply of water is as cool and fresh as it comes, flowing from the Allt an t'Sluic spring, high in the Drumochter hills.

The distillery

Dalwhinnie is in the heart of the Highlands, in what is officially the highest spot for a distillery in Scotland at an altitude of a little over 1,000 feet. It is surrounded by the Grampians and the Cairngorms, and overlooks tributaries to the Spey. Despite its remote location, however, it has had considerable money spent on its visitor centre, and attracts a steady stream of guests. It is one of Diageo's original six "classic malts", and it is just that – one of the truly great Highland malts.

Visiting details

It's testament to the popularity of this malt that so many people make the trek to this remote and lofty distillery. But the view from here is exceptional. Ring ahead before you go, particularly in winter, when there are fewer tours. The visit includes a glass of whisky, and the admission charge is redeemable against the purchase of a bottle in the shop.

must know

Contact details
Dalwhinnie, Inverness-Shire
01540 672219

www.malts.com

Core range
Dalwhinnie 15-year-old
Distillers Edition 1986
 Double Matured

Signature malt
Dalwhinnie 15-year-old:
whisky's answer to a Harlan
Coben crime novel, twisting
its way into and out of taste
cul-de-sacs at breathtaking
pace, before reaching an
unexpected but totally satisfying
climax. Earthy, smoky, swampy,
overwhelming – a thoroughly
recommended whisky.

Dalwhinnie
Distillery

Edradour

Region: Highlands

Sited within easy reach of the main cities, Edradour attracts an amazing 100,000 visitors a year, with only Glenturret, home of The Famous Grouse Experience, able to boast better numbers.

The distillery

The popularity of Edradour as a visitor attraction is remarkable, given the fact that it is one of Scotland's smallest distilleries. It makes just 12 casks of whisky a week, and getting hold of it is not always easy. But Edradour's whisky commands huge loyalty from those who have discovered it, particularly if they have visited the site.

Edradour is independently owned by the bottler Signatory, which is headed up by Andrew Symington. The distillery has launched a whole host of strange and unusual whiskies, many of which are bottled straight from the cask, and is also experimenting with peat levels and unusual finishes.

Visiting details

Edradour is Scotland's smallest distillery and produces whisky in the most traditional manner possible. Free tours are offered, and few distilleries enjoy greater popularity because of the intimate and personal nature of the visiting experience. The distillery is open all year round.

must know

Contact details
Pitlochry, Perthshire
01796 472095

www.edradour.co.uk

Core range
Edradour 10-year-old
Edradour Straight from
  The Cask range

Signature malt
Edradour 10-year-old

Go on, treat yourself...
Edradour 30-year-old

Fettercairn

Region: Highlands

Fettercairn was licensed in 1824, making it one of the oldest legal distilleries in Scotland. But it has had a mixed history, and to this day it has been something of a misfit as a single malt.

must know

Contact details
Laurencekirk, Kincardineshire
01561 340205

www.whyteandmackay.co.uk

Signature malt
Fettercairn "1824" 12-year-old

The whisky

Taste-wise, Fettercairn isn't as weighty as many of its Highland neighbours and its unassertiveness has meant that it has been overlooked by many as a single malt. Most of the output here goes into Whyte & Mackay's blends, where its unusual taste profile seems to excel.

Visiting details

Fettercairn's visitor centre has been open for nearly 20 years, but it is not in an obvious tourist location and it attracts a modest number of visitors. It's open from May to September, Monday to Saturday. Tours are conducted for adults twice a day and there is a small charge. Groups can be accommodated if a booking is made in advance. Visitors have the chance to fill their own bottle with a distillery-only 15-year-old from a sherry or an American oak cask.

Glencadam

Region: Highlands

When it closed in 2000, Glencadam looked like it had gone for good, but just three years later it was bought by Angus Dundee Distillers and brought back to life.

The distillery

Although now owned by Angus Dundee, as under its previous ownership, most of Glencadam's whisky is destined for a range of blends, including Ballantine's, Teacher's and Stewart's Cream of the Barley.

However, Glencadam is something of a hidden gem, and the release of a 15-year-old from the distillery was welcomed in a number of quarters. That's not at all surprising, because it's an extremely drinkable and pleasant malt.

Visiting details

Glencadam is open to visitors on Monday to Thursday afternoons. Visits are by appointment only, and the distillery can only cater for small groups.

An independent bottling of Glencadam 16-year-old

Glendronach

Region: Speyside

Shut for six years between 1996 and 2002, Glendronach's reprieve came in the form of demand for the Ballantine's blend, to which the distillery contributes some of the malt content.

must know

Contact details
Forgue, near Huntley
01466 730202

Core range
Glendronach 12-year-old
Glendronach 33-year-old
Vintage 1968

Signature malt
Glendronach 12-year-old:
rich in red berry fruit flavours
and intense malt.

Go on, treat yourself...
Glendronach 33-year-old:
sherry cask perfection, with
toffee, Crunchie bar and a
mouth-watering wood and
malt balance. Stands up to
its age robustly.

The distillery

Beyond supplying Ballantine's, current owners Pernod Ricard are planning even greater things for Glendronach, which looks set for a new lease of life. The distillery is a traditional one – with wooden washbacks, almost exclusive use of ex-sherry casks and stone dunnage warehouses for maturation – and the new owners are likely to make a virtue of that fact. Despite attempts to keep the stills coal-fired, however, European Union regulations have recently forced them to convert to oil.

Visiting details

The distillery offers two tours a day, Monday to Friday – one in the morning and one in the afternoon. There's a video presentation too, the opportunity to try the whisky at the beginning and end of the tour, and the chance to see an old floor maltings.

Glenfarclas

Region: Speyside

Glenfarclas is still owned and run by the Grant family, but there is nothing small-scale and domestic about its operation, which is that of a progressive and successful international business.

The distillery

Despite the competitive demands of a global market, there is still something wonderfully traditional and old-fashioned about Glenfarclas. While every other distillery seems to be marketing their whiskies with "special finishes", for example, Glenfarclas doesn't bother. It eschews any form of gimmickery, focusing instead on its strengths – malts produced in top quality sherry casks. Like The Macallan, Glenfarclas makes robust whiskies that stand up well to long sherry ageing, so it's not uncommon to find drinkable Glenfarclas that has been aged for more than 40 or 50 years. Few other distilleries would be able to match that.

Visiting details

Glenfarclas has a bustling and pleasant visitor centre that is open all year round but with reduced hours during the winter months. There are regular tours of the distillery. Before you go, check their website to see if there are any vouchers being offered – such as for a complimentary dram for visitors of a special bottling like the distillery's 25-year-old.

must know

Contact details
Ballindalloch, Banffshire
01807 500209

www.glenfarclas.co.uk

Core range
Glenfarclas 10-year-old
Glenfarclas 12-year-old
Glenfarclas 15-year-old
Glenfarclas 21-year-old
Glenfarclas 25-year-old
Glenfarclas 30-year-old
Glenfarclas 105

Signature malt
Glenfarclas 12-year-old:
more fruit and oak than the 10, and slightly stronger, but still with the lashings of sweet malt that the distillery's famed for.

Go on, treat yourself...
Glenfarclas 30. Rich, fruit cake chewiness and lots of chocolate and orange. Wonderful.

Glenfiddich

Region: Speyside

Glenfiddich is the single malt that lit the touch paper to start the malt whisky explosion. It began in the 1960s and, in the UK at least, "Glenfiddich" soon became synonymous with "malt whisky".

The distillery

Glenfiddich's owner, William Grant, was not only the first company to promote a single malt, but was also the first to open up the secrets of the malt world by opening a visitor centre. No fan of malt whisky should ever forget that, and nor should this whisky be dismissed as a novice's whisky, just because it has been around so long. It has maintained its position as the world's biggest selling malt for good reason.

Glenfiddich's owner has continued to invest in the distillery to make sure that it still has a home worthy of its world status, and everything here is stylish and impressive. And because Glenfiddich shares a site with the traditional and more "serious" malt distillery Balvenie, there is something here for both novice and seasoned enthusiast.

Visiting details

A brand new visitor centre, shop and restaurant ensure that Glenfiddich stays at the top of its game. It's an elegant and visitor-friendly distillery, and offers tours in a number of languages.

The Cooperage at Glenfiddich Distillery

must know

Contact details
Dufftown, Banffshire
01340 820373

www.glenfiddich.com

Core range
Special Reserve 12-year-old
Caoran Reserve 12-year-old
Solera Reserve 15-year-old
Ancient Reserve 18-year-old
Glenfiddich 30-year-old

Signature malt
Special Reserve 12-year-old:
no frills fruity Speysider with the drinkability factor turned up high. Often dismissed as an entry level malt, every whisky 'expert' should revisit it from time to time to remind themselves just how good it is.

Go on treat yourself...
The rich, soft and lush chocolate flavours in the 30-year-old are worth seeking out.

Glen Garioch

Region: Highlands

Glen Garioch sits alone, a few miles off the road from Aberdeen to Speyside. It doesn't tend to garner the same kind of attention that its sisters Auchentoshan and Bowmore receive.

The distillery

Glengarioch's pot stills

Remember the charismatic loner at school – the one who was a little weird yet aroused curiosity nevertheless, and when you got to know him was really interesting? Welcome to Glen Garioch, whisky's enigmatic loner.

Okay, it may not be quite as strange as all that, but Glen Garioch (pronounced "Glen Geery") is a quirky little distillery that produces a whisky that's hard to pin down. This is partly because there are peated and unpeated versions, but there are also distinctive notes to Glen Garioch that are uniquely its own.

Visiting details

The distillery is small and intimate. It's open from Monday to Friday and offers tours every hour. The tour guides the visitor through every stage of production, ending with a dram of Glen Garioch at the visitor centre. You can also fill your own bottle and personalise the label. VIP tours of the distillery are available, too, and need to be booked in advance.

must know

Contact details
Meldrum, Aberdeenshire
01651 873450

www.glengarioch.com

Core range
Glen Garioch 8-year-old
Glen Garioch 15-year-old
Glen Garioch 21-year-old

Signature malt
Glen Garioch 15-year-old:
an excellent introduction to a
Highland malt – a touch of oak
and smoke around a mass of
malt, and with green fruit and
a distinctive Glen Garioch
earthiness.

Go on, treat yourself ...
If you can find it you should go
for the Glen Garioch 46-year-
old 1958, the oldest Glen
Garioch produced. Only a
handful of bottles still remain.

Glengoyne

Region: Highlands

Lying a few miles outside Glasgow, this is a friendly and transparent distillery, offering some of the most in-depth tours and experiences available anywhere in Scotland.

The distillery

Glengoyne's pretty, 200-year-old distillery is set in a wooded area that has associations with Rob Roy, and it is one of the few surviving distilleries in this part of Scotland. Unchallenging, clean and pure tasting, Glengoyne whiskies are easy to drink and ideal for the novice. However, an extensive range of older and vintage malts guarantees a challenge for the more experienced palate, too.

Visiting details

The four-hour Glengoyne Masterclass is unique in Scotland. It includes a comprehensive guided tour of the distillery and bonded warehouses, presentations on various aspects about whisky production, a whisky-blending session and tastings. At the end of the visit, guests are presented with a 200ml bottle of their created blend, a personalised bottle of Glengoyne 10-year-old Single Highland Malt, and a Glengoyne Masterclass label, certificate and cellar book. Alternative tours focus on specific subjects, such as blending or cask tasting.

must know

Contact details
Drumgoyne, near Killearn
01360 550254

www.glengoyne.com

Core range
Glengoyne 10-year-old
Glengoyne 12-year-old
 Cask Strength
Glengoyne 17-year-old
Glengoyne 21-year-old
Glengoyne 28-year-old

Signature malt
Glengoyne 10-year-old: clean, crisp fruity malt that shows off all the distillery characteristics.

Go on, treat yourself...
The 16-year-old Scottish Oak, if you can get it, or the 21-year-old, which has a rich sherried quality and some deep, fruity, almost blood orange, notes.

Glen Grant

Region: Speyside

Glen Grant is an enigma. It sits in the pretty whisky village of Rothes in the heart of Speyside, but it has a personality and charm like no other in this region, and its whiskies can be elusive.

The distillery

Named after the family that founded it in the 19th century, Glen Grant Distillery is situated in outstanding gardens created more than 100 years ago by Major James Grant. The grounds include a delightful whisky safe by a little bridge, where the Major is reputed to have courted fair maidens.

The whisky itself is pale and young. Bottles of Glen Grant are sold by the millions in mainland Europe, particularly in Italy, but surprisingly little is seen elsewhere. However, the distillery acquired new owners in 2006, when the Italian drinks giant Campari entered the world of whisky, and it may be that more of this distillery's output will reach British and American shelves in the future.

Visiting details

The gardens alone at Glen Grant are worth visiting, while the distillery itself offers tours from late March until the end of October. Children are not permitted into the production areas.

must know

Contact details
Rothes, Morayshire
01542 783318

Core range
Glen Grant (no age)
Glen Grant 5-year-old
Glen Grant 10-year-old
Lord of the Isles

Signature malt
Glen Grant: clean and crisp, like a green apple.

Go on, treat yourself ...
Gordon & MacPhail have some Glen Grant that's been aged for more than 30 years – well worth exploring!

**The gardens at
Glen Grant Distillery**

Glenkinchie

Region: Lowlands

Glenkinchie represents the Lowlands in drinks consortium Diageo's original Classic Malts range. Its gentle personality makes it an ideal aperitif whisky.

must know

Contact details
Pencaitland, Tranent,
East Lothian
01875 342004

www.discovering-distilleries.com

Core range
Glenkinchie 10-year-old
Distillers' Edition 14-year-old

Signature malt
Glenkinchie 10-year-old: light and easy with a hint of ginger.

The distillery

With Edinburgh just a bus ride away, Glenkinchie is the nearest thing the Scottish capital has to its own malt, and it would be all too easy to dismiss this as a token malt – light, refined and suitably easy on the palate to reflect the more genteel face of Scotland. It is, however, a quality whisky, with a dry, spicy finish.

The close proximity to Edinburgh and the presence of the on-site museum ensure that a healthy number of tourists pass through Glenkinchie's gates every year, which is important, as there are few Lowland distilleries left.

Visiting details

The distillery has a visitor centre, but perhaps the main reason to visit is the Museum of Malt Whisky Production, which is housed in the old maltings and includes old distillery tools. The collection even includes copper "dogs" – containers designed to smuggle out stolen spirit, which vary from tubes that would go down the trouser leg to elaborate breast plates. The distillery is open most of the year; hours and days vary, depending on the season.

Glenkinchie's pot stills

Glenlivet

Region: Speyside

The first licensed distillery in Scotland is also one of its best.
As a place to visit, as a producer of exceptional whisky and in
historical terms too, Glenlivet has very few rivals on Speyside.

The distillery

Glenlivet's owner, Pernod Ricard, wants the
distillery's malt to challenge Glenfiddich for the
number one spot worldwide, and the distillery is
growing its core brands accordingly. However, the
company has also to satisfy the thirst of enthusiasts
for rarer malts from the archives, making the
distillery both commercial and esoteric. Glenlivet has
even let its whisky veteran Jim Cryle have his own
mini-still, so that twice a year he can distil spirit in
the way that it would have been 200 years ago.

What a great combination: a distillery with
superb whisky; a couple of enthusiastic eccentrics
at the helm; and enough tales of derring-do in
the distillery's history to fill a *Boy's Own*
annual several times over.

Visiting details

The Glenlivet has one of the best visitor
centres in Scotland, with a warm fireside
seating area, informal shop, café and an
interactive exhibition. It is open Monday to
Saturday from the end of March until the
end of October, and tours are free. They
include a complimentary whisky at the end.

> **must know**
>
> **Contact details**
> Ballindalloch, Banffshire
> 01542 783220
>
> www.theglenlivet.com
>
> **Core range**
> The Glenlivet 12-year-old
> The Glenlivet 15-year-old
> French Oak Reserve
> The Glenlivet 18-year-old
>
> **Signature malt**
> The Glenlivet 18-year-old:
> not only a signature malt but
> also classic Speyside, with rich
> apple and berry fruits, and
> clean, fresh malt.
>
> **Go on, treat yourself ...**
> The French Oak Reserve is
> wonderful, but if you're at a
> duty-free shop stocking the
> Nadurra 16-year-old, that's
> the one. Look for the cask
> strength version, with
> lashings of malt, chocolate
> and spice.

Glenlivet 25-year-old

Glenmorangie

Region: Highlands

Some distilleries just drip with style and class, and this is one of them. If you're wanting to really spoil yourself, stay in a country house nearby and live like a laird for a little while.

must know

Contact details
Tain, Ross-shire
01862 892477

www.glenmorangie.com

Core range
Glenmorangie
 10-year-old Original
Glenmorangie Artisan Cask
Glenmorangie 18-year-old
Glenmorangie 25-year-old
Glenmorangie Nectar D'or

Signature malt
Glenmorangie 10-year-old
Original: complexity, spice and
oak dance around the malt with
gay abandon and thrilling effect.

Go on, treat yourself...
Limited edition Glenmorangie
Margaux Cask Finish Vintage
1987: whisky making at its finest,
and a must for any fan of this
distillery. Bursting with flavour,
subtlety and vim.

The distillery

First, visit the spring that releases its precious water after a few hundred years permeating through rock, then marvel at the time and dedication the distillery puts into making its whisky. Glenmorangie may be one of the giants of whisky, and therefore taken for granted by some, but it is also among a handful that spare no expense in sourcing the finest oak in which to mature their whisky. The quality of the malt here is going from strength to strength and, to highlight that fact, the distillery overhauled its range in late 2007. With its rugged coastline and bracing breezes, just being around this distillery makes you feel healthy and vital, too. Though quite a long trek north, it is, without a doubt, well worth the effort.

Visiting details

Glenmorangie offers free tours of its highly impressive distillery and a discount off some of the more expensive bottles. There is also a visitor centre and a museum.

Glenmorangie
Nectar D'or

Glen Moray

Region: Speyside

Hidden away at the end of an unremarkable town street, Glen Moray has been overshadowed by its more illustrious sisters, Ardbeg and Glenmorangie. That, however, may be set to change.

The distillery

Glen Moray's dedication to a fine wood policy is starting to pay off handsomely. If its relatively new owners, LVMH, can halt the pointless cycle of discounting and devaluing the distillery's less expensive malts, then some of the more niche bottlings coming out of this definitive Speyside distillery will get the full credit they deserve.

Visiting details

Glen Moray is a small distillery, but offers a pleasant and personal tour for a minimal cost. Starting at the new visitor centre, the tour includes access to warehouses, where perspex-ended casks allow a rare opportunity to see the spirit as it matures and develops colour. The "Fifth Chapter" tour is altogether more comprehensive, and gives participants the chance to sample rarer whiskies. The manager's house is now used for events and tastings, further developing the distillery's appeal.

must know

Contact details
Elgin, Speyside
01343 550900

www.glenmoray.com

Core range
Glen Moray Classic
Glen Moray 12-year-old
Glen Moray 16-year-old
There is also a range of
vintages and distiller's
choice bottlings

Signature malt
Glen Moray 12-year-old:
classic Speyside whisky with
fruit, honey and malt all in
balance. Simple, but
beautifully executed.

Go on, treat yourself...
The 1991 Mountain Oak Malt
The Final Release: spicy,
warming and richly sweet,
with a hint of ginger.

Glen Ord

Region: Highlands

Glen Ord is one of Diageo's biggest producing distilleries, but it is something of a journeyman malt, and a succession of name changes has done little to help it build a reputation and following.

The distillery

In the past few years, changes have happened again, and it may be that a bottle of traditional Glen Ord will become worth buying as a collector's item before long. The reason for the change came about because Diageo decided to target the Asian markets, where The Macallan has long been dominant. To compete, Diageo needed a sherried whisky to rival Macallan's, so the sherry cask content in Glen Ord has since been upped, and the whisky rebranded for Taiwan as The Singleton of Glen Ord. Hopefully this is a one-off, and not the start of a trend that will see malts specifically focused on certain territories in the same way that blends are marketed.

must know

Contact details
Muir of Ord, Ross-shire
01463 872004

www.discoveringdistilleries.com

Core range
Glen Ord 12-year-old

Visiting details

The distillery lies to the north of Inverness, so it's a fair trek. Like The Dalmore and Balblair, however, the region makes the effort of visiting worthwhile, and the whisky doesn't disappoint either. Glen Ord is open throughout the year, but hours vary considerably by season. There is a charge, which is redeemable against the purchase of a 70cl bottle.

Glen Ord Distillery

Glenturret

Region: Highlands

"Which is Scotland's most visited distillery?" would make a great pub quiz question. And the answer: Glenturret, a distillery well-placed for tourists and with great visitor facilities.

The distillery

Glenturret has a fine pedigree. It was founded in 1775 and may well be the oldest working distillery in Scotland. It is small, producing about 300,000 litres per year, and most of the output goes into The Famous Grouse, which is the best-selling blend in Scotland. That doesn't leave much whisky for single malt bottlings, but, unusually, the distillery does offer vatted (blended) malts, aged at 12, 18 and 30 years. It's fair to assume that the other whiskies included in the vatting come from Glenturret's sister distilleries at Highland Park and Macallan.

Visiting details

Glenturret, which is open most of the year, is home to The Famous Grouse Experience *(see also p111)*, an excellent interactive offering that includes a room where films are projected in three dimensions – one film offers the sensation of flying over Scotland on the back of a grouse! The distillery is quite small, and the combined effect of its cottageyness and the state-of-the-art visitor experience is rather like dressing a farm labourer in a space suit.

must know

Contact details
Crieff, Perthshire
01764 656565

www.famousgrouse.co.uk

Core range
The Glenturret 10-year-old

Signature malt
10-year-old: rich, bold and honeyed, with a strong malt backbone.

Go on, treat yourself ...
The Whisky Exchange in London and Douglas Laing have both released 27-year-old independent bottlings.

Highland Park

Region: Islands

Orkney is a long way to go to visit a distillery, but Highland Park meets all expectations, and drinking a dram in the cosy visitor centre when the rain is lashing down is one of life's great pleasures.

The distillery

The Orkney Islands are a strange mix of stone circles, First and Second World War memorials, and prehistoric villages. It's a harsh and unforgiving place, but with tremendous soul. The distillery is traditional and cottagey, and has its own floor maltings. Some of its malt is kilned over fires fuelled by peat dug from nearby fields. As for the whisky: it is, of course, exceptional, and nowhere can it be enjoyed more than at the distillery itself, especially when the wind is up and rain batters the windows.

Visiting details

With its own maltings and imposing peat fires, Highland Park is a treat. There are tours every half an hour from April to October, and one afternoon tour from November to March. The gift shop is open throughout the year.

must know

Contact details
Kirkwall, Orkney
01856 874619

wwww.highlandpark.co.uk

Core range
Highland Park 12-year-old,
15-year-old, 16-year-old,
18-year-old, 25-year-old,
30-year-old

Signature malt
Highland Park 12-year-old: soft fruits wrapped in honey and rounded off with a gentle smokiness. Excellent balance.

Go on treat yourself...
The 18-year-old: arguably the most balanced and complete malt of them all, with the trademark honey, malt and fruit given an extra dimension by the presence of wood, smoke and spice. Startling stuff.

Highland Park 30-year-old

Jura

Region: Islands

Though it often seems to be rather in the shadow of the whisky metropolis across the water on Islay, Jura is a top-notch distillery and produces a very fine malt in its own right.

The distillery

When flamboyant Indian entrepreneur Vijay Mallya bought Whyte & Mackay in 2007, he said that his dad would have been particularly proud, because in the deal he had acquired Jura Distillery, which produced his father's favourite Scotch. It wasn't an acquisition based on sentimentality, though. As Mr Mallya put it, " you can be nostalgic over a few million pounds, but not a few hundred million".

In addition to the distillery's usual output, Jura occasionally likes to release a peated malt, just to prove it can bark as loudly as its neighbours across the water on Islay, if it so chooses. A very young peated Jura is definitely worth seeking out.

Visiting details

You have to be determined to visit Jura. It means either crossing by plane (expensive) or ferry to Islay, then taking a small ferry across the raging waters to reach an island populated mainly by deer and adders. Not surprisingly, therefore, when you do arrive, you are made most welcome. Jura is a lovely distillery and is open most of the year (though it shuts for one month each year so ring in advance). Tours are free and there's a complimentary dram at the end.

Jura Distillery

Knockdhu

Region: Speyside

The distillery is called Knockdhu, but, because it was often confused with nearby Knockandu, owners Inver House decided to call the single malt by its Gaelic name, anCnoc ("the hill").

The distillery

Knockdhu is a substantial distillery, and a high proportion of the output goes towards its single malt. Though often classed as a Speyside whisky, Knockdhu is adamant that its style is that of a Highland malt. Its complex, earthy and clean taste owes much to the traditional way in which the whisky is made. It is the operator and not a computer who decides when to start collecting the whisky, and the spirit is condensed in worm tubs – Knockdhu is one of only a handful of distilleries still to use this method.

Visiting details

There are no visitor facilities at the distillery, but tours can be made by prior arrangement.

Knockdhu Distillery

Lagavulin

Region: Islay

Along with Ardbeg and Laphroaig, Lagavulin completes a "holy trinity" of distilleries in southeast Islay that have perfected the smoky and phenolic style of whisky for which the island is famous.

The distillery

Like Ardbeg and Laphroaig, Lagavulin has the sea lapping at its doorstep and is everything you'd hope that a distillery should be. And Lagavulin's warehouses are among the most atmospheric you'll find anywhere in Scotland.

In recent years, Lagavulin suffered some major stock shortages, and its absence made many hearts grow all the fonder. No-one has ever doubted its quality, but the shortages have given it what can only be described as an iconic status.

Visiting details

Lagavulin is one of Islay's "big three" distilleries, which are sat side by side on the shoreline, producing heavily peated whiskies. The distillery is open all year round, and tours are conducted regularly – though you should phone ahead to book a time slot.

Lagavulin Distillery

must know

Contact details
Port Ellen, Islay
01496 302730

www.malts.com

Core range
Lagavulin 16-year-old
Lagavulin 12-year-old
 Cask Strength
Distiller's Edition Double Matured

Signature malt
Lagavulin 16-year-old: a tidal wave of peat, oil and spices with a powerpack support of chewy malt. A masterclass in peat working at different levels.

Go on, treat yourself ...
Lagavulin 12-year-old Cask Strength: it's becoming very rare, but this super-charged and younger version of the classic 16-year-old is an altogether feistier, fuller and more challenging whisky.

Laphroaig

Region: Islay

Laphroaig is probably the most iconic Islay brand – the Marmite of whisky, which you either love or hate. If you love it, you tend to really love it, and few other malts can compare.

The whisky

First impressions of Laphroaig (pronounced "Laff-roy-g") are that it's all smoke, fish and medicine. But spend some time with it, and there is an impressive array of flavours behind the Vesuvian-like sardine and smoke attack. As an entry level malt, try the Quarter Cask. This is a whisky finished in smaller casks, accelerating the maturation and softening the peat attack to great effect. If you want to walk the tightrope without a safety net, then Scotch doesn't get much better than the 10-year-old Cask Strength. Also look out for special bottlings, such as to celebrate the annual Islay Malt and Music Festival.

Visiting details

With the sea lapping up to the distillery walls, Laphroaig is a stunning distillery to visit. It is small, informal and traditional in its methods, and the tours are undertaken by very knowledgeable staff. They are conducted twice a day, Monday to Friday, and if you call a day or so ahead, that's normally enough notice. The distillery usually closes in July and August.

Macallan

Region: Speyside

Famed for its attention to detail, its refusal to cut corners and for the quality of its sherried whiskies, The Macallan has long enjoyed a loyal and passionate following.

The distillery

Macallan really became the complete package when it launched its Fine Oak range just a few years ago. By combining sherry and bourbon casks, The Macallan has reined in the dominant winey notes and created a clean, fresh and sophisticated range of whiskies. The distillery itself is beautiful, set high on an estate overlooking the Spey. At its centre is Easter Elchies House, an imposing manor house now used to entertain guests. The still house is highly impressive, with small squat stills like beer-bellied penguins.

Visiting details

The distillery is open most of the year, though for reduced hours from November to Easter. It also shuts over Christmas and during the "silent" season through most of July. The standard tour includes a glass of 10-year-old, but you can also opt for the "precious tour", which costs more but includes a tasting of five Macallan malts. Both tours include a visit to warehouse 7, an interactive museum that shows the crucial role played by wood in whisky production.

Macallan 18-year-old

Oban

Region: Highlands

Oban is a wonderful mix of "Highlands and Islands". The approach is along the rugged west coast, which offers stunning scenery before you reach the bustling sea port – gateway to the islands.

The distillery

Oban's distillery is in the heart of the pretty sea port town, hidden away up a little side street. Its facilities are squeezed into the tightest of spaces, making it a cosy distillery with which it's very easy to fall in love. It drips with character and charm, and still uses worm tubs to cool the spirit from the stills, making for a characterful final whisky. The coastal location and the distinctive peatiness of the malt makes it one of the finest highland distilleries to visit. Oban is also an ideal place to drop by en route to distilleries on the islands or up north, further into the Highlands.

Visiting details

The distillery conducts tours, but is shut in January and has severely reduced hours in December and February. In 2008, it is introducing a new sensory and flavour experience, where a guide will lead participants to plot the progress of the spirit from wash to finished whisky. Those taking part will be able to taste the new make spirit and cask strength maturing whisky taken straight from the barrel.

must know

Contact details
Oban, Argyll
01631 572004

www.malts.com

Core range
Oban 14-year-old
Oban 1980 Distillers Edition
 Double Matured
Oban 32-year-old

Signature malt
Oban 14-year-old. A growling, purring vehicle that moves up the gears from gentle start to rich, fruity and reasonably smoky monster. Full and intriguing.

Oban
Distillery

Pulteney

Region: Highlands

Wick sits on the northernmost tip of Scotland, so Pulteney is the UK's most northerly mainland distillery. It's a no-frills operation in the heart of a rugged town that looks to the sea for its livelihood.

The distillery

You don't need much of an imagination to picture the locals cosying up with a drop of Scotch in Wick's bars on storm-swept winter nights. The whisky is tailor-made for the purpose, too, with maritime notes in abundance. If you venture to the distillery, you will be joining a pretty elite group, but as a result can expect a very warm reception and a generous glass of whisky for your trouble.

Under current owners, Inver House Distillers, Old Pulteney's range has been repackaged and the whisky's profile raised. The distillery often has special distillery-only bottlings available too, which have been excellent, making a trip here all the more worthwhile. The single cask offering takes some beating!

Visiting details

A full distillery tour, a shop and a visitor centre await those who make it so far north. The distillery is open from April to December, 10am to 3pm, and for restricted hours from January to March. Call in advance to book a place on the tour, and, once there, take the opportunity to personally bottle some whisky.

must know

Contact details
Wick, Caithness
01955 602371

www.oldpulteney.com

Core range
Old Pulteney 12-year-old
Old Pulteney 17-year-old
Old Pulteney 21-year-old

Signature malt
Old Pulteney 12-year-old: an outstanding tangy, salty seaside character and plenty of Highland bite; a rich whisky and a very more-ish one.

Go on, treat yourself...
The 17-year-old: Citrus fruits, rich malt and the trademark salt with some spice make this very hard to resist. For a treat, this is not too pricey either.

**Old Pulteney
12-year-old**

Royal Lochnagar

Region: Highlands

Royal Lochnagar is Diageo's smallest distillery and one of its prettiest, nestling on the edge of the Balmoral estate, the Scottish home of the Royal Family.

must know

Contact details
Balmoral
01339 742700

www.malts.com

Signature malt
Royal Lochnagar 12-year-old

Go on, treat yourself...
From time to time, a special Selected Reserve Royal Lochnagar is released. It is a limited edition release, often aged for about 20 years.

The distillery

Royal Lochnagar is one of only three distilleries entitled to use the prefix "royal". This is as a result of the fact that Queen Victoria visited the distillery in 1848 and took a liking to it.

The distillery, which is used as a training base for Diageo employees, ticks all the right boxes when it comes to the romance of whisky. Cottagey in character, it maintains many of the old traditions and equipment of whisky making, including wooden washbacks and "worms" – flat-lying copper pipes for condensing the spirit that pass snake-like through a pool of cool water on the roof of the distillery. Two small stills and a long fermentation period contribute to a distinctive and weighty Highland whisky.

Visiting details

Tours are conducted throughout the year, with reduced hours in winter. Children under eight are not allowed in the production areas. This is one of the most traditional distillery tours, whereby small groups are guided through the production process. For those wanting a more advanced experience, there are tutored tastings available if booked in advance.

Royal Lochnagar Distillery

Speyburn

Region: Speyside

A hidden gem of a distillery with a history stretching back to 1897, Speyburn was designed by the great distillery architect Charles Doig, who created a very compact building.

The distillery

Speyburn lies in the heart of Speyside. The district is verdant and beautiful, and Speyburn's pagoda-style chimneys make it an archetypal Speysider. It is, however, surrounded by far better-known distilleries. Much of Speyburn's malt is exported to America, and it is not particularly well known in its own right in Europe. But it has been well looked after by the current owner, Inver House Distillers, and we may hear more of it in the future.

Visiting details

There are no visitor facilities at Speyburn, but a personal tour of the distillery and warehouses can be made by prior arrangement.

must know

Contact details
Rothes, Speyside
01340 831213

www.inverhouse.com

Core range
Speyburn 10-year-old
Speyburn 25-year-old
 Solera Cask

Signature malt
The 10-year-old: clean and simple, sweet and with the faintest smoke undertow.

Go on, treat yourself...
The 25-year-old Solera Cask: not an easy whisky to pin down because its style is evolving. But what you can expect is the age showing through, with the Speyburn sweetness being tempered by spice and oak from the wood.

Springbank

Region: Campbeltown

Campbeltown was once a thriving centre for whisky production. In the mid-19th century, it was home to 34 distilleries and became known as the "whisky capital of the world".

must know

Contact details
Campbeltown, Argyl
01586 552085

www.springbankdistillers.com

Core range
Springbank 10-year-old
Springbank 10-year-old 100 Proof
Springbank 15-year-old
Springbank 25-year-old

Signature malt
Springbank 10-year-old, 100 Proof: a full malt like no other; blatant and colourful, on the one hand; nuanced, unpredictable and engaging, on the other.

Go on, treat yourself...
Springbank 32-year-old: rare now, but those who have tasted it speak in reverential tones about its jammy and woody qualities, and its coconut notes.

The distillery

Campbeltown's decline in the early 20th century was rapid, and by the mid-1930s there was only Springbank and Glen Scotia left. Today, Glen Scotia produces whisky only intermittently – historically with the help of Springbank.

Having said that, things are a little more productive in Campbeltown than that may suggest. Springbank, in fact, is a "three whiskies" distillery. In addition to the eponymous malt, Springbank also produces a limited amount of Longrow, a significantly peated whisky, and Hazelburn, which is triple distilled. And, since 2004, Springbank has also had a sibling called Glengyle – the first new distillery in Campbeltown for 125 years. It produces a malt called Kilkerran.

Visiting details

This is a traditional distillery that isn't really geared up for welcoming tourists. Nevertheless, with growing interest in the distillery, Springbank does now conduct tours all the year around, with the proviso that they are booked in advance.

Strathisla

Region: Speyside

This is one of the prettiest of all the Speyside distilleries, with archetypal pagoda chimneys and elegant surrounds. Visiting here is a little like arriving at a luxurious country hotel.

The distillery

The approach to the distillery is a delight; the beauty and tranquillity of the environment worth the journey alone. Strathisla is suffused with history, so it will come as no great surprise to discover that this is the oldest working distillery in the Highlands.

The distillery itself is beautifully maintained, but the overall highlight must be the maturation warehouse, which contains some of Chivas Brothers' oldest stock. A small fenced-off area within the warehouse contains rare and special casks, including one owned by Prince Charles.

Strathisla is a fine whisky and it plays a key role in the outstanding Chivas blend. This distillery is a fitting home for such a refined brand.

Visiting details

After a welcome in the dram room, dominated by leather sofas, you're given a choice of Strathisla or Chivas to drink. During the visit, shortbread and coffee are served, and every visitor receives a souvenir booklet. There is an admission charge, but this is still a great value-for-money tour.

must know

Contact details
Keith, Banffshire
01542 783044

www.chivas.com

Core range
Strathisla 12-year-old
Strathisla 18-year-old

Signature malt
Strathisla 12-year-old: rich, sherried and satisfying, with a nice platform of sweet fruits.

Go on, treat yourself...
Strathisla 15-year-old Cask Strength: bolder, oakier and arguably drier than the standard bottling, and not very common. The extra strength gives it added depth.

Strathisla 12-year-old

Talisker

Region: Islands

Nestling among the rocky crags and rugged shoreline of Skye, Talisker is in perfect harmony with its desolate surroundings. So too is its whisky, which reflects the wild, stark landscape.

The whisky

Skye is a rugged and unforgiving island, which has witnessed some of the country's bloodiest and most dramatic history. Traditionally, its climate has been harsh and challenging. Unsurprisingly, then, there's an earthiness about the people and the place. But there's an other-worldliness to Skye, too, as if you have been transported to another planet. Both the distillery and the whisky echo this environment, and Talisker is a bold and confident malt – and very masculine. Talisker 18-year-old was voted the best malt in the world in the first World Whisky Awards, organised by *Whisky Magazine* in 2007.

Visiting details

Talisker is another distillery that takes some reaching but rewards those who do make the trip. It is worth spending a few days on Skye, and the distillery is open most of the year, though with reduced hours in winter. There is a charge for the tour, but you get to taste one of the world's truly iconic spirits and the cost is redeemable against a purchase in the shop.

must know

Contact details
Carbost, Isle of Ske
01478 614308

Core range
Talisker 10-year-old
1986 Distillers Edition Double Matured
Talisker 18-year-old
Talisker 25-year-old

Signature malt
Talisker 10-year-old: classic pepper and smoke explosion; a dry storm of a whisky.

Go on, treat yourself ...
Talisker 18-year-old: this has everything – lots of smoke, the trademark pepper and spice, a honeycomb heart and a three-dimensional, chunky depth not present in the 10-year-old. It is whisky at its most wonderful.

Talisker
10-year-old

Tobermory

Region: Islands

Over the years and under various owners, whisky from Tobermory has been bottled as a single malt, a blend and a vatted malt – all under the same name and in near-identical bottles!

The whisky

Now, thankfully, the distillery produces a clearly marked 10-year-old single malt (a clean and pleasant whisky), which has to be matured on the mainland because the distillery's warehouses were sold off and converted into flats. The distillery also produces a peated version, which goes by the name of Ledaig (pronounced "Led-chig"). It is starting to build a powerful name for itself and, unusually for a malt, is very good when young.

Visiting details

The distillery itself is sited by the beach in a pretty town that is home to the children's TV series *Balamory*. It's a small and compact place, where visitors are welcomed with a short film before embarking on a tour. If you do visit, seek out a third version of the malt: Iona Athol, which is a vatting of Ledaig and Tobermory, and is sold only on Mull and nearby Iona. The distillery is open to visitors from Easter to the end of September from Monday to Friday, and there are regular tours. At other times of the year, visits can be made by appointment.

must know

Contact details
Tobermory, Isle of Mull
01688 302645

www.burnstewartdistillers.com

Core range
Tobermory 10-year-old
Ledaig 10-year-old

Signature malt
Tobermory 10-year-old:
light and refreshing, with a blemish-free hit of malt through its heart.

Go on, treat yourself ...
1972 Ledaig: if you can find it, this is a huge, world-class whisky; as perfect a combination of sherry wood and peat smoke as you are ever likely to find.

Tobermory Distillery

Tomatin

Region: Highland

Built in 1897, Tomatin really hit its stride in the mid-20th century, when it embarked on an expansion plan that eventually took it to production levels of 12 million litres per year by the early 1970s.

The distillery

In 1974, Tomatin was the biggest producer in Scotland. It still has the capacity to produce a significant five million litres of spirit each year, yet Tomatin is a strange beast, and is not as well known as perhaps it might be. The main reason for this is because most of its whisky goes abroad, either as single malt or, more commonly, through a number of blends, most notably The Antiquary. Occasionally, the distillery bottles vintage expressions, which are worth seeking out. In the past few years, there have been bottlings from 1973 and 1965.

When it was acquired by Japanese shareholders in 1986, Tomatin became the first Scottish distillery to be under Japanese ownership.

Visiting details

Tomatin might not be the prettiest of distilleries, but its owners have invested in the visitor facilities and it attracts a healthy number of tourists each year.

must know

Contact details
Tomatin, Inverness-Shire
01808 511444

www.tomatin.com

Signature malt
Tomatin 12-year-old:
a balanced and easy-going,
yet full Highland whisky.

Tomatin
12-year-old

Tullibardine

Region: Highlands

Tullibardine had been mothballed for nine years when a consortium came together to buy it and its stocks in 2003. They then set about marketing Tullibardine to great effect.

The distillery

Because the distillery was not producing for so many years, the first releases since Tullibardine's reopening have come from the archives and include some whiskies that are more than 30 years old. The marketing of the whisky shows a modern approach, coupled with a strong emphasis on heritage (the shop and café are called 1488, to highlight the fact that beer was brewed on the site more than 500 years ago). Tullibardine's owners are quite prepared to try out new approaches. Special finishes – even a beer finished in whisky casks – have been released. It's a way forward that appears to be working, and the distillery is now exporting across the world.

Visiting details

The concept of distillery visits is absolutely core to what Tullibardine is all about. The distillery is part of a shopping complex designed to attract the flow of tourists on the A9, and it offers a range of visitor experiences. For whisky enthusiasts, the best of these would be the "connoisseurs' tour", guided by the distillery manager.

must know

Contact details
Blackford, Perthshire
01764 682252

www.tullibardine.com

Signature malt
Tullibardine 10-year-old

Other visiting experiences

In recent years whisky tourism has become a serious business, and you don't necessarily have to go to a working distillery to find out about malt production. There are several visitor centres that are dedicated to the broader picture of whisky making.

Dallas Dhu
Forres, Morayshire • 01309 676548
www.historic-scotland.gov.uk
Dallas Dhu is a closed distillery lying in the heart of Speyside. It was purchased by Historic Scotland and has been maintained as a visitor attraction. As no whisky is produced here, it operates under a different set of health and safety rules to a working distillery, and this means that visitors can get closer to the machinery involved in whisky production, which is what the whole experience is geared towards. Dallas Dhu is open all year round, but with reduced hours during winter.

Dewar's World Of Whisky
Aberfeldy Distillery, Aberfeldy, Perthshire
01887 822010 • www.dewarswow.com
Dewar's is one of the world's most established blended whiskies, and Dewar's World of Whisky has become one of Scotland's top tourist sites. Based at the Aberfeldy Distillery to the north of Perth, it operates as a separate facility to the distillery and is a modern and interactive family experience. It tells the story of the Dewar family and explains the skills of the whisky blender. There are a range of tours available, from a relatively modest and basic one to the stylish Signature Tour, which includes a tasting of five whiskies, including a 21-year-old Aberfeldy and the wonderful and expensive world-class blend Dewar's Signature.

Dewars's World of Whisky, at Aberfeldy Distillery

The Famous Grouse Experience

Glenturret Distillery, Crieff, Perthshire • 01764 656565
www.famousgrouse.co.uk

Conveniently situated just off the A9 at Glenturret Distillery, the Famous Grouse Experience has helped ensure that this is Scotland's most visited distillery. It is an enticing combination of quaint old distillery and state-of-the-art, interactive visitor attraction. The three-dimensional projection room is great, with images that glide across the floor and walls. At one point, the floor even appears to be a frozen river, complete with cracking ice!

**The Famouse
Grouse emblem**

The Museum of Malt

Glenkinchie Distillery, Pencaitland, East Lothian
01875 342005 • www.discovering-distilleries.com

About 145 miles from Edinburgh, where the Firth of Forth meets the sea, is Glenkinchie Distillery, the Lowland representative in Diageo's original Six Classic Malts series. Glenkinchie launched a Museum of Malt Whisky 40 years ago, making it something of a pioneer, and today the exhibits include a beautiful distillery model made 80 years ago, and an impressive array of distillery tools and equipment.

Glenkinchie's pot stills

The Scotch Whisky Heritage Centre

354 Castlehill, The Royal Mile, Edinburgh • 0131 220 0441
www.whisky-heritage.co.uk

Situated at the top of the Royal Mile, near Edinburgh Castle, this is another interactive attraction. It's recently been renovated, though the tour still explains the history of Scotch whisky and the process by which it is made. Children can enjoy a barrel ride through history and meet a ghost, while adults can learn the distinctions between single malt, grain, vatted and blended whisky. And, of course, there's a dram to be had too.

Allt-a-Bhainne

Region: Speyside

Seagrams built Allt-a-Bhainne along with Braeval Distillery in the 1970s. Their construction was to help meet the growing demand for blended whisky, and Allt-a-Bhainne has only ever been a provider of malt for blends. Consequently, its fate has been tied to that of blended whiskies per se. It was mothballed in 2002 but reopened three years later when current owners Pernod Ricard needed more malt to expand output of its newly acquired Chivas Regal brand.

Allt-a-Bhainne is a large distillery, producing an estimated four million litres of spirit each year, and is designed to operate with the minimum number of people. There are no official malt bottlings, but some malt is occasionally bottled independently.

Ardmore

Region: Highlands

Ardmore annually produces about five million litres of malt. It is mainly destined for the Teacher's blend, but an increasing amount is released as a single malt. As at sister distillery Laphroaig, some of Ardmore's whisky is matured in quarter sized casks to develop the malt flavour further. Although Ardmore doesn't currently offer tours, a visitors' centre is planned for 2009.

As for the whisky, Ardmore Traditional Cask is a peated malt that enjoys the highest quality maturation – first in ex-bourbon barrels and then in traditional quarter casks.

Ardmore Traditional Cask

Aultmore

Region: Speyside

Only a tiny fraction of the whisky produced at Aultmore is bottled as a single malt, with the vast majority being used for blending purposes. Unsurprisingly, then, this is a clean, consistent no-nonsense malt. The distillery started producing in 1897 and has been in demand pretty much ever since.

There is not much Aultmore around as single malt, but if you are interested in exploring this whisky further, it would be worth seeking out some independent bottlings, such as those produced by Elgin-based bottlers Gordon & MacPhail.

Aultmore's stills

Balmenach

Region: Speyside

Balmenach produces whisky exclusively for blending, so there are no single malt bottlings released from the distillery – though owners Inver House qualify the above statement with the words "as yet", so the situation may change in the future. It's a sizeable operation, nevertheless, with capacity for the production of two million litres of spirit each year, some of which finds its way into independent bottlings from time to time.

Although there are no visitor facilities at Balmenach, the distillery manager will take people round the plant by prior arrangement.

Balmenach Distillery

Benrinnes

Region: Speyside

This is another of Diageo's production distilleries, producing malt for a range of blends, and with little whisky released as single malt. It produces a healthy 2.6 million litres of spirit each year.

There are technical points of interest at Benrinnes. It is one of just a handful of distilleries using the "worm tub" method to condense the spirit. The method is so named because of the worm-like horizontal pipes which lie in a tank of cool, flowing water. The other unusual feature is that its six stills are arranged in two groups of three, with one wash still feeding two spirit stills.

Craigellachie

Region: Speyside

The village of Craigellachie is situated in the very heart of Speyside, alongside the rivers Spey and Fiddich. For many years the main hotel in the village has been seen as a base camp for all good whisky expeditions. The Craigellachie distillery itself is not very exciting, though – its featureless glass front and garish red lettering are suggestive of a factory rather than a malt producer. Very little Craigellachie is bottled as single malt, most being used by Dewar & Sons.

Dewar's Craigellachie Distillery

Dailuaine

Region: Speyside

Founded in 1852, Dailuaine has been in almost continuous production for 155 years, except for three years between 1917 and 1920, when it was closed due to fire damage. With the potential to produce more than three million litres of spirit a year, Dailuaine is one of Scotland's biggest malt contributors, yet one of its least known. That is because only a small percentage of the spirit made here makes it into single malt bottlings; most is used for Johnnie Walker blends.

must know

Contact details
Aberlour, Banffshire
01340 872500

www.malts.com

Signature malt
Dailuaine 16-year-old

Deanston

Region: Highlands

Deanston Distillery

Deanston Distillery is capable of producing about three million litres of whisky a year, with much of the output going into the respected Scottish Leader blended whisky. Less than a fifth of the spirit ends up as a single malt and – not to put too fine a point on it – there hasn't been much to write home about it in the past. If ever there has been a "journeyman malt", this has been it. However, the signs are that the 12-year-old is on the up, and some experts observe a marked improvement in the last two or three years.

The distillery at Deanston is a relatively modern facility, built in the 1960s on the site of an old cotton mill that was designed by the architect and inventor Richard Arkwright in the late 18th century.

must know

Contact details
Deanston, nr Doune, Perthshire
01786 841422

Signature malt
Deanston 12-year-old: reliable rather than flashy, with clean honey and malt notes.

Go on, treat yourself...
Deanston 30-year-old Single Malt Limited Edition: a veritable old gent, but the years in cask have given it great depth, with a tangy, spicy edge.

Dufftown

Region: Speyside

Diageo's biggest producer at Dufftown makes about four million litres of whisky each year, the majority destined for Bell's. The distillery has been expanded several times in the last 30 years, and it has one of the longest fermentation periods of any whisky – up to 120 hours. Only a very small amount whisky from Dufftown Distillery is ever released as single malt.

must know

Contact details
Dufftown, Keith, Banffshire
01340 822100

www.malts.com

Signature malt
Flora & Fauna 15-year-old

Go on, treat yourself ...
Singleton of Dufftown

**Dufftown malt is
used in Bell's
blended whisky**

Glenallachie

Region: Speyside

Glenallachie was founded in 1967 and has been a sizeable contributor to a range of blended whiskies ever since. It was the last distillery to be designed by the great distillery architect of the 20th century, William Delmé-Evans, who died in 2002.

Its current lifeline was established in 1989, when Pernod Ricard took over. Single malt bottlings are rare, but a cask strength version aged for about 15 years was released in 2005.

must know

Contact details
Aberlour
Banffshire
01542 783042

Glenburgie

Region: Speyside

Glenburgie is a tale of two eras. The original distillery, dating from 1829, hit top gear in the late 1950s, when it was expanded to help meet the demand for malts to put into blended whisky. It housed two Lomond stills – tall pot stills with plates in the neck designed to alter the reflux of the still. However, the Lomond stills were very hard to maintain, and ceased to be used. Malt produced at this time occasionally appears under the name Glencraig.

The modern era began in 2005, after the distillery had been rebuilt at a cost of more than £4 million. Bottlings are very rare but worth seeking out, with gingery and dark chocolate charateristics offering an unusual and pleasing experience.

must know

Contact details
Forres, Morayshire
01343 850258

Glendullan

Region: Speyside

The Glendullan Distillery can produce 3.7 million litres a year, yet it is virtually unknown as a single malt whisky. In recent times, its main claim to fame was as one of the malts that were mixed with Cardhu to turn that single malt into a controversial and short-lived vatted version, Cardhu Pure Malt.

A 12-year-old Glendullan was available for a while, and some is sold as an 8-year-old through supermarkets. It was chosen as the Speaker's whisky by Betty Boothroyd, Speaker of the House of Commons, in 1992, and there was a special bottling to celebrate the distillery's centenary in 1997.

must know

Contact details
Dufftown, Keith, Banffshire
01340 822100

www.malts.com

Go on, treat yourself …
All the Glendullan Rare Malts are worth tasting, but they are relatively difficult to find.

Glendullan 12-year-old

Glen Elgin

Region: Speyside

must know

Contact details
Longmorn, Elgin, Morayshire
01343 862100

www.malts.com

Signature malt
Glen Elgin 12-year-old

Go on, treat yourself...
Glen Elgin 32-year-old

Few distilleries have had a more rocky existence and survived to tell the tale. Opened at the beginning of the 20th century, just as the industry was falling in on itself, Glen Elgin was closed and sold four times over in its first six years. It did survive, however, and was first officially bottled as a single malt in the 1970s. The distillery attracts attention from enthusiasts because it has six worm tubs for condensing the spirit – a slow method, but one that produces a characterful whisky.

Besides a few special bottlings that Diageo have released, Glen Elgin is most closely associated with the White Horse blend.

**Glen Elgin
12-year-old**

Glenlossie

Region: Speyside

must know

Contact details
Elgin, Morayshire
01343 862000

www.malts.com

Signature malt
Flora & Fauna 10-year-old

Glenlossie is something of an oddball distillery. It sits next door to another distillery, Mannochmore, and shares the same workforce and warehouses. It operates only between October and March, though its output is highly rated by whisky blenders.

Glenlossie is a rarity as a single malt but is highly regarded for its outstanding quality, so look out for any independent bottling.

Glenrothes

Region: Speyside

Although Glenrothes has no visitor centre, it does let visitors have a look around, on occasion, if the visit is arranged in advance. The distillery is a pretty one, sited in the centre of Rothes, and there's lots of great history associated with the distillery too. It's a big producer, providing whiskies for several blends, including Cutty Sark. The single malt is the epitome of sophistication and style. It is packaged in distinctive, grenade-shaped bottles with hand-written labels. The whisky is excellent, and if you want Speyside fruit and honey with the volume turned up to 11, this is the distillery to seek out.

Glenrothes Select Reserve 1994

Glen Scotia

Region: Campbeltown

Campbeltown on the west coast of Scotland used to be a rich and vibrant whisky-producing region. It saw no fewer than 34 distilleries set up here in its 19th-century heyday. Now just two are producing whisky for the market, Glen Scotia and Springbank, with four-year-old Glengyle set to become the third. Now run by Loch Lomond Distillery Company, Glen Scotia produces only 750,000 litres a year, making it one of Scotland's smallest producers. Though a relatively rare malt, if you can track down an independent bottling, it will be something to treasure.

Glen Spey

Region: Speyside

There is considerable debate among Speyside lovers as to which town is the spiritual capital of the region. Certainly Rothes, rich in history and blessed with four working distilleries, has a strong case to argue. The least known of the four Rothes distilleries, Glen Spey is one of those Diageo Speyside workhorses that make malt primarily for the blended whisky market – in this case, particularly for J&B. Although single malt bottlings are rare, there have been a number of independent releases and, a few years ago, a 12-year-old was released in Diageo's Flora and Fauna range.

Glentauchers

Region: Speyside

Another of the many anonymous but sizeable producing distilleries now owned by Pernod Ricard in Speyside. After a chequered and unimpressive history, it reopened under the ownership of Allied Domecq in 1992, since when it has been producing 3.4 million litres of spirit a year for inclusion in Ballantine's blended whisky. Ballantine's was acquired in 2005 by Pernod Ricard, who have ambitious plans for this internationally well-known blend, so Glentauchers' future would seem secure as one of its key malt suppliers. Single malt bottlings remain very rare, even though several whisky writers rave about the Glentauchers malt.

**Glentauchers
Distillery**

Inchgower

Region: Speyside

Inchgower has the capacity to produce a sizeable amount of whisky – in excess of two million litres – but most of it is used for Diageo's heavyweight blends, including Bell's and Johnnie Walker. It's a pretty distillery, situated near the coast in the north of the Speyside region; the coastal proximity might explain why it's not a typically sweet Speysider.

Diageo has released a 22-year-old and 27-year-old as part of its Rare Malts series, both of which are excellent.

Inchgower
14-year-old

Kininvie

Region: Speyside

Kininvie is one of Scottish whisky's best-kept secrets. It is hidden away behind Glenfiddich and Balvenie distilleries, and, although its owner William Grant & Sons has talked about releasing a single malt from Kininvie, it has yet to happen. The distillery's purpose is to provide malt for blending, and, so far, it has been fully employed in this pursuit. Perhaps, now that the company has opened a new malt distillery to ensure supplies in the future, there will be sufficient whisky at Kininvie for it to be bottled in its own right.

Kininvie malt goes into William Grant & Sons' blends, such as Monkey Shoulder blended malt whisky.

Knockando

Region: Speyside

must know

Contact details
Knockando, Aberlour, Banffshire
01340 882000

www.malts.com

Core range
Knockando 18-year-old,
plus various other vintages
without age statements.

Although regarded as an elegant and complex whisky, Knockando has only had a very small presence in the single malt market in the UK. On the Continent and in America, however, it is more widely distributed. Un-aged single malt bottlings do appear in the UK from time to time, and in some markets older expressions of Knockando are released. The malt is also one of the key whiskies in the J&B blend.

Knockando Distillery

Linkwood

Region: Speyside

must know

Contact details
Elgin, Morayshire
01343 862000

www.malts.com

Core range
Linkwood 12-year-old

Signature malt
Linkwood 12-year-old:
more floral than fruity; wispy,
subtle and rounded.

Linkwood is one of the most attractive and intriguing distilleries in the whole of Scotland. The whisky is highly respected; the distillery location, surrounded as it is with a nature reserve, is quite wonderful; and the strange production set-up keeps the trainspotters in business for hours.

There are two sets of stills on site: one set produces the bulk of the spirit, while an older set is employed for some of the year to produce a different spirit; the two are then mixed before filling to cask. Linkwood's distinctive whisky is particularly popular among blenders, while rare bottlings of single malt, whether official or through the independent sector, are much sought after by a hardcore band of devotees.

Loch Lomond

Region: Highlands

Loch Lomond is like no other distillery in Scotland, and has more in common with one of the large Irish or Canadian distilleries, with pot stills, a grain plant and "rectifiers" all employed to make a range of different whisky styles, most of which are used for the company's own blends.

The reason for producing so many types is to help overcome shortages of malt, a problem that may well be reappearing for independent blenders as demand for whisky rises. So Loch Lomond, Old Rhosdhu (sometimes bottled as a surprisingly youthful 5-year-old) and Inchmurrin all hail from here.

must know

Contact details
Alexandria, Dumbartonshire
01389 752781

www.lochlomonddistillery.com

Longmorn

Region: Speyside

Longmorn is the whisky equivalent of a cult French-language film – adored by aficionados of the cinematic art; often ignored in other quarters. Or, at least, that was the case. Owner Pernod Ricard seemed content to allow the whisky's reputation to rest on the back of some outstanding independent bottlings until a few years ago, when a cask strength 17-year-old was released. That has since been followed by an official 16-year-old release.

The distillery opens its doors on occasions, such as during the Spirit of Speyside Festival, held on the weekend of the first British May bank holiday.

**Longmorn
16-year-old**

must know

Contact details
Elgin, Morayshire
01542 783042

Signature malt
Longmorn 16-year-old: a rich, complex and weighty malt; and, at 48% abv, a big hitter all round.

Go on, treat yourself...
Longmorn 17-year-old Distillers Edition: a masterpiece at cask strength – an oral pillow fight as fruit, oak and barley all battle for supremacy. Stunning!

Macduff

Region: Speyside

must know

Contact details
Macduff, near Banff
01261 812612

Core range
Glen Deveron 10-year-old
Glen Deveron 15-year-old

Signature malt
Glen Deveron 10-year-old

Confusingly, the small amount of single malt produced by Macduff Distillery is bottled under the name Glen Deveron, which alludes to the local river. The distillery was opened in the 1960s to provide blending stock, notably for William Lawson, but the malt is worthy of investigation in its own right because it is atypical of Speyside whiskies.

Macduff pot stills

Mannochmore

Region: Speyside

must know

Contact details
By Elgin, Morayshire
01343 862000

www.malts.com

Signature malt
Mannochmore 12-year-old

Mannochmore was established in 1971, it having been built to help provide malt for the Haig blend during a boom time for whisky. Consequently, Mannochmore is a rare beast as a single malt.

The distillery is famed for having produced the "black whisky" Loch Dhu, a decidedly average whisky that is, nevertheless, still in demand among collectors. An empty bottle recently sold on EBay for £80, and when independent retailer The Whisky Shop released some Loch Dhu from its vaults, the bottles were selling for £175.

Miltonduff

Region: Speyside

Miltonduff is another of the great distilleries formerly owned by the Canadian whisky giant Hiram Walker. The distillery's purpose remains primarily to produce blending malts. It went through a period of using Lomond stills – which were designed to produce an array of different styles of malt from the same still. The experiment was abandoned because Lomond stills are inefficient and notoriously difficult to clean, but, while they operated, the whisky produced was known as Mosstowie, bottles of which do appear from time to time. These days, Miltonduff has the capacity to produce more than five million litres of malt, making it a big player, and it is a key component of Ballantine's. The distillery was acquired in 2005 by Pernod Ricard, which has since made Miltonduff its trade and production headquarters.

must know

Contact details
Elgin, Morayshire
01343 547433

Mortlach

Region: Speyside

Whisky enthusiasts adore Mortlach. It has a complex and unique distillation process that includes a motley crew of stills and a partial triple distillation, which ensures that all sorts of compounds are kept in the mix to give the whisky a variety of subtle nuances that are unlike anything else in the region. Blenders love Mortlach too, and it is widely considered to be an "adhesive malt" that can bring lots of other flavours to order. The distillery is sizeable, and capable of producing three million litres of spirit a year. A very small amount of 32-year-old Mortlach was released a few years ago.

must know

Contact details
Dufftown, Banffshire
01340 822100

www.malts.com

Signature malt
Mortlach 16-year-old:
a flavour-rich, chunky, oily and quirky malt, which tastes like nothing else on Speyside.

Royal Brackla

Region: Highlands

Royal Brackla is situated in Cawdor, home of the
famous castle that features in Shakespeare's
Macbeth. It is approaching its 200th anniversary,
having opened in 1812, and it is one of only three
distilleries able to use the word "Royal" – an honour
granted in this case because William IV was rather
partial to Brackla's whisky.

Most of the production here goes for blending,
but some whisky writers have commented on the
strong bourbon
characteristics found
in older, independent
bottlings of Brackla.

Royal
Brackla

Scapa

Region: Islands

Until a couple of years ago, Scapa was an extremely
rare whisky. The distillery was all but abandoned,
producing spirit for only a few weeks a year to top
up supplies. However, it was refurbished and put
back into production four years ago. When
Pernod Ricard then took it over from Allied
Domecq, the distillery continued to receive
support, though plans for a visitor centre and
regular tours were put on hold.

Look out for some of Scapa's older and
cask strength expressions, which have a
barley intensity and some salt and peat
notes that generate a rewarding
level of complexity.

Scapa
14-year-old

Speyside

Region: Speyside

This is a neat and compact distillery, a long way to the south of the area most associated with Speyside but, nevertheless, close to a major tributary of the Spey River. The distillery was used for the filming of the *Monarch of the Glen* TV series, but, in terms of whisky making, it is something of a secret to many.

Speyside produces a range of malts, and the company has its own Glasgow-based operation for blending and bottling its whisky. It is not a big player in the UK, and it's fair to assume that a great deal of the distillery's whisky goes abroad.

must know

Contact details
Drumguish
01540 661060

www.speysidedistillery.co.uk

Core range
Drumguish
Speyside 8, 10 and 12-year-olds

Signature malt
Speyside 12-year-old:
the richest and fullest of the distillery's malts.

Strathmill

Region: Speyside

Strathmill is one of those classic and traditional distilleries that ticks all the boxes when it comes to the romance of malt. It is a pretty distillery, with twin pagoda chimneys, situated by the side of a river in the town of Keith, the epicentre of Speyside.

It's a sizable distillery, which includes in its production process a purifier that's designed to produce a light style of whisky, much in demand for blending – particularly for J&B. A 12-year-old single malt was released for the first time in 2001, as part of Diageo's Flora and Fauna range.

must know

Contact details
Keith, Banffshire
01542 883000

www.malts.com

Signature malt
Strathmill 12-year-old

Tamdhu

Region: Speyside

Tamdhu is the least known of Edrington's working distilleries – the others being Highland Park, Macallan, Glenrothes and Glenturret. Tamdhu has a major role to play, however, and, with the capacity to produce more than four million litres of spirit per year, it is a key contributor to blends such as The Famous Grouse. It is also the only distillery still using "saladin boxes", the commercial method for malting barley, and Tamdhu can provide malt for the group's other distilleries.

A 29-year-old independent bottling of Tamdhu

Teaninich

Region: Highlands

Diageo has a number of Speyside distilleries that operate in the shadows, and none more so than Teaninich. Close to the relatively famous Dalmore *(see p77)*, Teaninich is a sizeable distillery capable of producing more than 2.5 million litres per annum, yet it is virtually unknown in its own right. The whisky has a couple of quirky production characteristics that are of interest to the technically-minded, but, for the most part, Teaninich slips under the radar. A bottling did appear in Diageo's Flora and Fauna range some years back, but otherwise, as a single malt, Teaninich is very much a rarity.

Tomintoul

Region: Speyside

It's a case of beauty and the beast: one of the prettiest regions of Scotland providing the backdrop for a factory distillery built in the early 1960s to make large quantities of spirit. Tomintoul can produce more than three million litres of spirit each year, and, since the turn of the millennium, it has been owned by independent bottler Angus Dundee. In that time, Tomintoul has been quietly building up its reputation as a single malt, and the 16-year-old is particularly impressive. The distillery has also launched a peated whisky called Old Ballantruan, and, along with BenRiach, is seriously challenging some preconceptions about the region.

Tomintoul 16-year-old

Tormore

Region: Speyside

Designed to be a showcase distillery, Tormore is an imposing place, with all sorts of curious features that deserve to be experienced, such as a musical clock that plays a range of traditional Scottish tunes, a belfry and a curling lake. Unfortunately, the distillery doesn't welcome visitors.

Tormore has become another sizeable producer of malts intended for blends such as Ballantine's and Teacher's. However, Pernod Ricard took over ownership recently, and the 12-year-old official bottling seems to be on the up. Hopefully, this delightful time capsule of a distillery will echo with the footsteps of visitors once more before long.

Tormore 12-year-old

Scotland's closed distilleries

Over the years, the demand for whisky has ebbed and flowed, and a close examination of the years in which new distilleries have been established gives a clear indication of the industry's boom years. The corollary of this is that, when demand is low, distilleries fall silent and are "mothballed" or closed entirely.

A pause for thought

In the current climate, things are on the up for whisky, and there are several new distilleries in the process of being built or that are already producing spirit which has yet to reach maturity. But, as they say, what goes up must come down, and the history of whisky production is scattered with the skeletons of great distilleries that have failed to survive periods when a cull has been necessary. There are whole books written on closed distilleries, many of which are much lamented by enthusiasts. Some former distilleries have taken on an iconic status.

You may well take the view that, with so many positives to talk about and so much new whisky reaching the shelves, it's not worth dwelling on the past and the ghosts of formerly great distilleries, now turned into shopping centres, town centre car parks or housing estates. But, while the buildings may have physically gone, some of the whisky may remain. Many of the big drinks companies maintain casks from closed distilleries and occasionally release bottlings, while independent bottlers often specialise in releasing whisky from a long-gone distillery.

A matter of time

Time is a key factor, though. Whisky supplies from closed distilleries dwindle further each year, as they become another year older and find themselves increasingly at the mercy of the cask. Eventually the wood will destroy the malt altogether; or, because whisky in Scotland gets weaker the longer it ages, the cask's contents will eventually slip under the minimum legal strength of 40% abv.

Such whiskies are clearly collectible, but, above this, in some cases they offer the enthusiast the chance to better understand a specific style of whisky. The Lowlands, for example, has very few distilleries left, but those long gone, such as Rosebank and St Magdalene, are considered to have produced classic Lowland style whiskies.

Many closed distilleries have been razed, but a few still stand empty, "mothballed" and potentially redeemable. In the recent past, BenRiach and Bruichladdich were reopened by independent companies after some years of being silent.

Some bottles are exceedingly rare, and all are reasonably so. Here is a guide to some closed distilleries and the bottles you may find in specialist whisky retailers. Three stars indicates exceptionally rare; one, less so; and two, somewhere in between.

BenRiach Distillery was reopened in 2004 after a two-year period in "mothballs".

A selection of closed distilleries

Banff (Speyside) ***
Closed in 1983 and demolished in 1985. Some casks have been released by independent bottlers and Diageo has small stocks left, but it was never commonly available as a single malt.

Ben Wyvis (Highlands) ***
Closed in 1977. Exceedingly rare and it will set you back a few hundred pounds if you go for a bottle.

Braeval (Speyside) **
Closed in 2002 but not demolished. The occasional independent bottling appeared in the early part of the millennium, and while Braeval is rarely found in its own right, Deerstalker 10-year-old is made using Braeval whisky.

Clynelish was built in the 1960s to replace the old Clynelish Distillery, which after a short period of closure reopened as Brora Distillery. Brora produced whisky for over a decade, finally closing for good in 1983.

Brora (Highlands) *

Closed in 1983 but still on the site where the Clynelish Distillery operates in the village of Brora. Different expressions have been released regularly in the last 10 years, and the Brora 30-year-old is one of the world's truly great malts.

Caperdonach (Speyside) *

Mothballed in 2002, but available officially as a cask strength 16-year-old. There have been various independent bottlings too.

Coleburn (Speyside) **

Closed in 1985 and sold to two brothers in 2004. Plans for a shopping hotel and music complex were never realised. Very hard to find, though a release in Diageo's Rare Malts series in 2000 can be found at very good retailers.

Convalmore (Speyside) *

Mothballed in 1985 and sold to William Grant in 2000 to be used as store warehouses. Independent bottlings and the occasional release from Diageo mean that it can be bought from about £50.

Dallas Dhu (Speyside) *

Closed in 1983 and sold to Historic Scotland in 1986. now a distillery museum *(see p110)*. Can be found through a number of independent bottlers.

Glen Albyn (Highlands) **

Stopped producing in 1983; demolished in 1986. A distillery bottling was released as part of the Rare Malts series in 2002 and there are some independent bottlings.

Glenesk/Hillside (Highlands) **

Closed in 1985. Some independent bottlings and the occasional release of both Hillside and Glenesk in Diageo's Rare Malts series.

Glen Flagler (Lowlands) ***

Closed in 1985 after just 20 years in production. Extremely limited and highly collectible.

Glenglassaugh (Speyside) *
Closed in 1986, but a 19-year-old released in 2006 is still available if you are willing to search for it; there have been other independent bottlings too.

Glen Keith (Speyside) *
Mothballed in 2000. It is possible to find Glen Keith on sale for about £30, and there are a number of independent bottlings. It's rumoured that the Craigduff and Glenisla releases from independent bottler Signatory come from Glen Keith.

Glenlochy (Highlands) **
Production stopped in 1983, and the distillery was demolished in 1992, since when it has been released in Diageo's Rare Malts series and through some independent bottlers.

Glen Mhor (Highlands) **
Closed in 1983 and demolished in 1986. There have been Rare Malts releases and some independent bottlings during the last six or seven years.

Glenugie (Highlands) ***
Closed in 1983. Some independent bottlings do exist, but they are few and far between.

Glenury Royal (Highlands) **
Increasingly difficult to find, though top retailers still have some. The Whisky Exchange has very old and rare bottles, if you've got the budget to match.

Imperial (Speyside) *
Mothballed in 1998, and there have been recent releases officially from Pernod Ricard and independent bottlers.

Inverleven (Lowlands) ***
Some independent bottlings are available.

Kinclaith (Lowlands) ***
Rarest of the rare. Closed in 1975, after less than 20 years in production. You'll do well to find any of this under £600, and you can expect to pay in excess of £1000.

Ladyburn (Lowlands) ***
Lasted less than 10 years before shutting in 1975. Just about unobtainable as Ladyburn, but Royal Mile Whiskies had a bottle called Ayrshire, which is meant to have come from this distillery.

Littlemill (Lowlands) *
Production stopped in 1992 and the buildings were mostly demolished four years later. An 8-year-old is quite common and in recent years there's been a fair bit of 12-year-old too.

Lochside (Highlands) **
Mothballed in 1992. Official bottlings are very rare and expensive, but you will find independent bottles at better retailers.

Millburn (Highlands) ***
Production ceased in 1985. Much of the equipment ended up at Benromach. Millburn has been released in the Rare Malts series and there is a small amount from independent bottlers.

North Port/Brechin (Highlands) ***
Mothballed in 1983 and demolished 10 years later. You'll find some independent bottlings priced around £50.

Pittyvaich (Speyside) **
Mothballed in 1993, officially closed in 2002, and increasingly difficult to find.

Port Ellen (Islay) ***
Closed in 1987 and arguably the most sought after of all closed distillery malts. You can get it if you're prepared to pay.

Rosebank (Lowlands) *
Closed in 1993. Has attracted the attention of independent bottlers, so you can find it.

St Magdalene (Lowlands) **
Closed in 1983. Some has been released by Diageo in the Rare Malts series and through independent bottlers.

Tamnavulin (Speyside) **
Closed in 1995. You can still get some reasonably-priced 12-year-old but, beyond that, it's pretty rare.

A Douglas Laing bottling of Port Ellen 25-year-old

Oddballs

If understanding whisky wasn't difficult enough, it's made considerably more so by the number of bottles that are released under a special name. Most frequently this is done to commemorate a one-off event, but it's not unheard of for a distillery to release a whisky just for its staff.

The quixotic world of whisky

Specially named bottlings may be released by the distillery or by an independent bottler. Some may even represent a particular style of whisky that was formerly produced at a distillery that has long since gone. In the case of Hazelburn whisky, for example, it is now made at the Springbank Distillery, while its name and style honour the Hazelburn Distillery, which closed down as long ago as the 1920s. The same distillery also produces a peated whisky called Longrow, which is not in the traditional Campbeltown style at all.

Longrow, a peated malt produced by Springbank Distillery in Campbeltown.

As one might expect with something as organic and dynamic as malt whisky, new distilleries may emerge at any time. Diageo is currently in the process of building a super-sized distillery in Speyside; the owners of independent bottler Duncan Taylor plan a distillery in the Speyside region also; and William Grant has built a new malt distillery close to its Girvan grain distilling plant in the southwest of Scotland.

Occasionally you might come across a whisky distillery that doesn't fit into any recognised category. What follows is a round-up of Scotland's newest distilleries, plus information about distilleries found elsewhere in the UK.

New distilleries in Scotland

Daftmill (The Lowlands)
The first spirit was distilled at Daftmill in 2004, and after three years of maturation became bona fide whisky in 2007.

Glengyle (Campbeltown)
Glengyle also celebrated the official birth of its whisky in 2007 as the spirit reached three years of age. The whisky may be some way off release yet, but it is to be called Kilkerran and will be the product of a range of cask types.

Kilchoman (Islay)
Now very close to reaching the all important third birthday, this micro-distillery brings the total on Islay up to eight.

Port Charlotte (Islay)
Make that nine. The owners of Bruichladdich are opening a distillery two miles up the road. In fact, they began distilling at Port Charlotte in 2001, and have been laying down peated whisky since then, so the first bottlings are on their way soon.

Distilleries elsewhere in the UK

While there has been talk of new distilleries in both Cumbria – for which a website exists heralding a Lakeland Distillery to be sited by the River Kent – and in Northumberland, there are only three sites producing whisky in England and Wales.

Penderyn (Wales)
The first malt from Penderyn was launched four years ago and now the distillery is successfully producing whisky and planning to increase its output.

The bottling plant at Penderyn Distillery

The Cornish Cyder Company (England)
This West Country cider company started producing an annual batch of whisky spirit some five years ago, and, although the early attempts were dodgy, recent distillations augur well. None of the whisky is available yet – they're planning for the long term – and pretty much all they have produced is pre-sold.

St George's Distillery (England)
James and Andrew Nelstrop, a father-and-son partnership, built this distillery from scratch in Norfolk. They bought their equipment from the renowned still manufacturer Forsyths in Scotland, and brought top whisky maker Iain Henderson down to operate it. Iain has since retired – again – and been replaced by a former Greene King brewer. The earliest date for bottling St George's whisky is the end of November 2009.

St George's Distillery will be bottling its first whisky in the next few years.

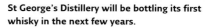

7 The fabulous fifty

With so many Scottish distilleries producing malt whisky, it comes as no surprise to learn that there are hundreds of different bottles to choose from – and the selection is constantly changing. Some expressions may be withdrawn, or run out because they were limited in the first place, while new bottles are continually being introduced. Here, we offer a summary of some of the very best Scotch whisky currently on the market.

Scotland's best whiskies

Here is a pick of what I consider to be the best Scotch whiskies currently available. Most of them have been released in the last three years, though one or two are evergreen personal favourites. As well as being strongly recommended, the list covers a diverse range of whiskies across the price spectrum.

Price guide

£	under £25
££	£26-50
£££	£51-80
££££	£81-125
£££££	over £125

Aberlour a'bunadh

The top fifty single malts

The recommendations here are not intended to be exhaustive, but to give a pointer to some of the best whiskies currently available from Scotland's wonderful distilleries.

● **Aberfeldy 21-year-old ££££**

Highlands 40% abv

Rich, full and fruity, with a nice wood and spice wrapping.

● **Aberlour a'bunadh ££**

Speyside 59.8% abv

Each batch of a'bunadh is slightly different, but the general character of the whisky is that of a big battering ram, with full marmalade fruit and a chewiness unmatched by any other malt.

● **Ardbeg Airigh Nam Beist ££**

Islay 46% abv

A growling rally car of a whisky – oil and smoke, with a sweet heart running through it.

● **Ardbeg Almost There ££**

Islay 54.1% abv

An untamed and fiery-tempered Ardbeg, completing the series of young and evolving Ardbegs with a flourish.

- **Ardmore Traditional Cask ££**

Highlands 46% abv

Intriguing. Initially savoury and earthy, but it evolves into something sweeter and fruitier. Grows on you.

- **Arran 10-year-old ££**

Islands 46% abv

A creamy, rich and deliciously fruity clean malt.

- **Auchentoshan 18-year-old £££**

Lowland 55.8% abv

Zesty, citrusy and elegant malt that carries its age and cask strength well.

- **Balblair 1977 ££££**

Highlands 46% abv

A distillery on the up? Clean, rich in fruit, and with an intriguing mix of fresh fruit, spices and a backbone of oak.

- **Balblair 1989 ££**

Highlands 43% abv

Fresh and tasty malt, with orange, raisins and sherry, and a full mouth feel.

- **Balvenie Roasted Malt 14-year-old ££**

Speyside 47.1% abv

Gorgeous spice and malt interplay, and a charming fresh fruit centre.

- **Balvenie 1972 Vintage Cask ££££**

Speyside 47.3% abv

Rich toffee, fruit, and a hint of smoke and spice.

- **BenRiach Fine Wood 15-year-old Madeira ££**

Speyside 46% abv

Classic Speyside with the volume turned up. A fruity starburst of flavours.

- **BenRiach Fine Wood 15-year-old Tawny Port ££**

Speyside 46% abv

Rich, warming, a tad spicy and a delightful finish.

Ardmore Traditional Cask

Balblair 1989

**Bowmore
18-year-old**

**Clynelish
14-year-old**

● **BenRiach Heredotus Fumosus ££**

Speyside 46% abv

Curious but engaging mix of smoky whisky finished in a Pedro Ximenez cask.

● **BenRiach Arumaticus Fumosus ££**

Speyside 46% abv

Best of the three Fumosus finishes, with complex dark cherry and cocoa notes from time spent in dark rum casks.

● **Benromach Organic ££**

Speyside 43% abv

Big, big hit of oak and orange liqueur up front, then fresh mouth-filling malt.

● **Bowmore 18-year-old ££**

Islay 43% abv

Replacing the much-loved 17-year-old but the mid peat and oak hit hold up well.

● **Brora 30-year-old £££££**

Highlands 56.3% abv

Increasingly rare, but a whisky to die for, with a delicatessen-like array of flavours and delicious smoke.

● **Bruichladdich Flirtation 20-year-old £££**

Islay 46% abv

As clean and breezy as malt gets, with raisin and fruity melon in the mix.

● **Bruichladdich Redder Still 22-year-old ££££**

Islay 50.4% abv

A rare beast: a complex whisky finished in a red wine cask – which works brilliantly.

● **Bunnahabhain 18-year-old ££**

Islay 43% abv

Best of the range, with deep creamy, fruity notes and a trace of brine, all held together by a balanced taste of malt and oak.

- **Bunnahabhain 25-year-old £££££**

Islay 43% abv

The wood's in the ascendency now, but the brine is still there and the overall result is a majestic and stately older whisky.

- **Caol Ila 25-year-old £££**

Islay 59.4% abv

Fantastic. Oil, lemons, peat and smoked fish. A Mediterranean meal in a glass.

- **Clynelish 14-year-old ££**

Highlands 43% abv

A fine and balanced Highland whisky, with just enough bite to elevate above the norm.

- **Cragganmore 12-year-old ££**

Speyside 40% abv

Ostensibly a Speyside malt, but there are all sorts of other subtle things going on that make it atypical. A mystery thriller with intriguing twist after intriguing twist.

Cragganmore
12-year-old

- **The Dalmore 1973 Cabernet Sauvignon £££££**

Highlands 45% abv

Spicy and tangy, with oranges and liquorice notes. Exquisite!

- **The Dalmore 40-year-old £££££**

Highlands 40.5% abv

The price reflects its rarity but, nevertheless, this is stunning – dark chocolate orange, wisps of smoke and some delightful spice.

- **Dalwhinnie 15-year-old ££**

Highlands 43% abv

Sugar and spice. Cocoa and peat under a rounded malt sheen. Try chilling it in the freezer and serving on a cold dessert, such as ice cream, with hot chocolate sauce!

- **Glencadam 15-year-old ££**

Highlands 40% abv

Savoury whisky with an earthy heart, lashings of malt and some complex undertones. A real grower.

Dalwhinnie
15-year-old

The Glenlivet
15-year-old
French Oak

- **Glenfiddich Vintage 1973 ££££**

Speyside 46.5% abv

Don't let familiarity breed contempt. This is a fine, full, citrusy megabeast of a malt that holds its head up high in any malt company.

- **Glenfiddich Toasted Oak 12-year-old ££**

Speyside 40% abv

Burnt toffee and vanilla, with a pleasant, spicy undertone. Lots and lots of flavour.

- **The Glenlivet Nadurra 16-year-old £££**

Speyside 57.2% abv

The cask strength version has a stunning mix of spices, giving the fruit and malt complexity and depth. Astounding!

- **The Glenlivet 15-year-old French Oak ££**

Speyside 40% abv

Some new French oak is used too, providing extra spiciness and giving the fruity, honeyed whisky a total makeover.

- **Glenmorangie Lasanta ££**

Highlands 46% abv

New look, new taste, but fine Glenmorangie with sherry wrapping and an enjoyable nuttiness.

- **Glenmorangie Nectar d'Or ££**

Highlands 46% abv

Heavy on the flavour, but the lemon, grapefruit and spice are attractive enough.

- **Glen Moray Fifth Chapter Distillery Manager's Choice £££££**

Speyside 59.6% abv

This distillery has been devalued, yet has the capability to produce some of the very best malt – such as this one.

- **The Glenrothes 1972 ££££**

Speyside 43% abv

Bold raisins, sherry and oak feature here, all married together with terrific élan.

The Glenrothes
Select Reserve

• The Glenrothes Select Reserve ££

Speyside 43% abv

A fruit bowl of flavours, with oranges, lemons and grapefruit popping up. You know you've been tangoed!

• Highland Park 16-year-old £££

Orkney 40% abv

Not a patch on the 18, but then what is? Still perfectly balances fruit, honey, smoke, oak and spice. Just not as loudly as its big brother.

Highland Park 16-year-old

• Isle of Jura 21-year-old £££

Islands 58.1% abv

Clean and fruity, sophisticated and very, very drinkable.

• Knockdhu anCnoc 12-year-old £

Highlands 40% abv

Almost too refined for its own good, but give it a chance and its mix of light smoke and sweetness can become beguiling.

• Lagavulin 16-year-old ££

Islay 43% abv

A true giant from the peated isle. A massive dose of peat on the nose; equally strong and smoky on the palate, with cocoa and liquorice, and a rich, deep growling body. Stunning!

Isle of Jura 21-year-old

• Laphroaig Quarter Cask ££

Islay 48% abv

An exceptional whisky from an exceptional distillery. Masses of peat and smoke, great chunks of malt and an overload of spice. Doesn't get better than this.

• Laphroaig 10-year-old Cask Strength ££

Islay 55.7% abv

Laphroaig with the thruster motors on. Massive peat attack, along with the richest malt and fruit double whammy found in any malt. Whisky's equivalent of Led Zeppelin: a battering ram on the face of it; a considered study in skill and sophistication on closer inspection.

Knockdhu anCnoc 12-year-old

Scapa
14-year-old

Talisker, where the
acclaimed 18-year-
old was produced

- **Laphroaig 27-year-old £££££**

Islay 51% abv

And another twist. This time it's plums, stewed strawberries
and liquorice in with the smoke. And a long, long finish.

- **The Macallan Fine Oak 15-year-old ££**

Speyside 40% abv

Best expression from the wonderful Fine Oak range. A stunning
mix of bourbon and sherry wood, and absolutely top drawer.

- **Old Pulteney 17-year-old ££**

Highlands 46% abv

Strong barley, lemon and grapefruit, along with spiciness from
the wood, make for a fine mix.

- **Scapa 14-year-old ££**

Islands 40% abv

Honey, brine and citrus in a surprisingly light and eminently
drinkable Orkney malt. Refreshing.

- **Talisker 18-year-old ££**

Isle of Skye 45.8% abv

Voted best malt at the World Whiskies Awards in 2007 and with
good reason. The trademark Talisker pepper and fire remains in
place, but the age gives it a sweeter third dimension. Faultless.

- **Tomintoul 16-year-old ££**

Speyside 40% abv

Smooth, rounded, complete and, with an array of changing
favours, my surprise discovery of 2007.

Blended whiskies

Outstanding quality isn't confined to single malt, and there are many great blended whiskies to be explored. Here is a selection of my personal favourites, followed by a list of what I consider to be the best blended (vatted) malts currently available.

Black bottle

- **Bailie Nicol Jarvie £**

Glenmorangie 40% abv

A fresh and gentle blend, with enough fruit to keep it interesting. A great introductory whisky and excellent value for money.

- **Ballantine's 17-year-old £££**

Chivas Brothers 43% abv

From an impressive range this is the pick: big mouth feel, lots of fruit and just enough prickling spice and oak to make it interesting yet confined by the smoothing grain. Masterful.

- **Black Bottle £**

Burn Stewart 40% abv

Probably the best-value Scotch whisky on the market. The perfect entry level malt for those exploring the wonderful world of peated whisky.

**Chivas Regal
25-year-old**

- **Chivas Regal 25-year-old £££££**

Chivas Regal 40% abv

A surprising slap of spice up front, then lashings of orange and then the most gentle of finishes that threatens to die away but doesn't. Exquisite and refined.

- **Dewar's Signature £££££**

John Dewar & Sons 43% abv

With very old Aberfeldy at its core, this would give most malts a run for their money. Combines a whisky rainbow of flavours that covers oak, malt, spice, fruit, smoke, honey and vanilla.

- **The Famous Grouse £**

Edrington Group 40% abv

The Kylie Minogue of blended whisky – decidedly mainstream and unchallenging, but very loveable and with the quality control

The Famous Grouse

**Hankey Bannister
21-year-old**

button set to maximum. Scores points for its mix of honey
sweetness and mildly abrasive edges.

• Hankey Bannister 21-year-old £££
Inver House 40% abv

As rounded as rounded gets, this is an easy-to-drink and
delightfully subtle mix that never lets you down. Special.

• Johnnie Walker Black Label £
Diageo 43% abv

The blenders' blend, this is the pick of the mainstream blends,
providing a delightful mix of flavours on a special smoky base.

• Macnamara Rum Finish £
Pràban/The Gaelic Whisky Collection 40% abv

Unusual to have a blend finished in another style of cask,
but the rum here gives a vibrant splash to a well-balanced
and rounded malt.

• Royal Salute 21-year-old ££££
Chivas Brothers 40% abv

Another distinguished name with a range of wonderful whiskies.
Delicious sweet vanilla and malt in perfect harmony.

• Whyte & Mackay 30-year-old £££££
Whyte & Mackay 40% abv

If you're going to spend big on a blend, you want something you
can't get elsewhere. This is the Moscow Philharmonic Orchestra
on a great night – faultless, note perfect and sensuously emotional.

• William Grant's Family Reserve £
William Grant 40% abv

**Johnnie Walker
Black Label**

Great value for money. Immense
flavour and a lovely one-two between
fruity malt and soft grain. Proof that
whisky doesn't need to break the bank.

**Royale Salute
21-year-old**

**William Grant's
Family Reserve**

Blended malt whiskies

Johnnie Walker Green Label

• Clan Denny Islay ££
Douglas Laing 40% abv

A mix of quality Bunnahabhain, Bowmore, Caol Ila and Laphroaig –
so a must for Islay fans. Peated sure, but given a richness from
the Bunnahabhain and Bowmore. Cracking!

• Compass Box: Oak Cross ££
Compass Box 43% abv

A spicy delight, and another big hitter for its price. New European
heads on old bourbon casks make for a unique and delightful mix.

• Compass Box: Peat Monster ££
Compass Box 45% abv

Growling Islay malts mixed with some old Speyside to produce a
honeyed, fruity and rounded, but still punchy, peated whisky.
All this company's range is good; this is excellent.

• Johnnie Walker Green Label ££
Diageo 43% abv

A mix of four malts and a refreshing, clean and thoroughly drinkable
session whisky. Minimum age 15, so it's great value for money.

• Monkey Shoulder ££
William Grant 40% abv

Aimed directly at the fashion scene, this is nevertheless a high-class
mix of three different malts, and has delightfully clean orange
and lemon notes at its heart.

• Serendipity ££
Moët Hennessy 40% abv

Now rare, but most intriguing – the accidental mix of very
old Ardbeg and young Glen Moray produced a wonderful
whisky (hence the name). The Ardbeg peat is tempered with
a packet of Starburst sweets in the middle.

Compass Box: The Peat Monster

8 Irish whiskey

Scotland might have established itself as the most famous whisky-producing nation on the planet, but it wasn't always so. Even now, other countries – and particularly Ireland – would state a case for producing spirits that match or better those produced by their Scottish cousins. The Irish have a long and proud tradition of whiskey-making (note the addition of the letter "e" for the Irish version of the drink), and over a drop or two they'll tell you that they invented the original drink (*uisce beatha* in Gaelic) and exported it to the Scots, who proceeded to make it in the "wrong" way.

Whiskey making in Ireland

The Irish will tell you that their whiskey is the genuine article, and that the Scottish version is rough and incomplete by comparison. And, should you require a little bricks-and-mortar proof of their contention, they'll point to the fact that the world's oldest licensed distillery is not in Scotland but in Ireland.

Bushmills Distillery

The cooperage at Bushmills

A grain of truth

Truth be told, the Irish version of whiskey history is not so clear cut. Like many such things, the roots of whiskey production are hard to pin down, and no-one can make a water-tight case for its birth. The Irish theory does have substance though, and should at least be considered seriously. The words *uisce beatha*, which spawned the word "whiskey", are from a Gaelic language common to the Irish and west coast Scots. Its entirely plausible that Irish monks travelled across the narrow stretch of water between the countries, ostensibly to win converts to Christianity. But it's very likely that they were in possession of distilling skills too, learned in the Middle or Far East, and that knowledge may well have been imparted alongside the religion.

It is also the case that, for a large part of the second millennium, it was Irish whiskey and not Scotch that was served to nobility and the educated elite. It took a sequence of misjudgements and disasters to reduce Irish whiskey from the powerful force it once was to the bit player it is today.

At key times, Ireland suffered partially self-inflicted wounds: it refused to export its whiskey to the

English, who turned to Scotland instead; a strong temperance lobby struck a severe blow to many distilleries; and it is also said that the Irish honourably upheld US Prohibition while the Scots made inroads into the American market by supplying illegal speakeasies. The Irish were dealt a further blow by the Second World War, when American servicemen got a taste for Scotch while serving in Britain.

By the 1960s many Irish distilleries had been forced to close, several more had amalgamated into one group called Irish Distillers, and the future of Irish whiskey looked in serious doubt. Irish whiskey is more expensive to make, too, because it is triple-distilled, giving it a further disadvantage in the modern era of high energy prices.

Thankfully, though, recent years have been kinder to the Irish whiskey industry, and there has been a renewed interest in the nation's whiskeys. This has been driven by Jameson, at the commercial end of the market, and by esoteric and niche whiskeys at the specialist end. With more competition within the Irish whiskey sector than there has been in years, and with a growing interest in traditional methods of

Jameson whiskey

must know

The word whiskey is a corruption of the Gaelic term uisce beatha, which is pronounced "ish-ka vah ". Just as the Scots spell whiskey differently to the Irish, they also use a variant spelling of the Gaelic, writing "uisge beatha" with a "g". It all means the same thing, though, "water of life".

Old Midleton Distillery is now preserved as a museum.

Cooley's pot stills

Greenore single grain whiskey

Clontarf single malt

The Millars blend

Michael Collins malt and blend

making whiskey, Ireland looks to have a healthy whiskey-making future once again.

What is Irish whiskey?

Your man in the pub buying you a glass or two will tell you that the main difference between Irish whiskey and Scotch is the fact that Irish whiskey is distilled three times, and single malt only twice. This is only partly true. There are distilleries in Ireland which distil just twice, and there are a couple of Scottish distilleries that do so three times.

He'll tell you that Irish barley is dried in kilns but never over peat smoke, unlike Scottish single malt. Not true: there are plenty of Scottish malts that have no peated barley in them, and there are a few Irish whiskeys that are made using peat (which is not surprising when you consider how much of the Emerald Isle consists of peat bog).

And finally, he'll tell you that Irish whiskey is pot still whiskey, which is unique to Ireland. And here he'd have a point, although now, sadly, only a fraction of Ireland's output is traditional pot still whiskey. As with Scotch, there are four styles of Irish whiskey.

Ireland produces a small amount of malt whiskey, which is produced in the same way as in Scotland; a very small amount of it is peated. There is a tiny amount of single grain whiskey also, triple distilled like much of the rest of Ireland's whiskeys. But it is the two other whiskeys produced by the Irish that sets the country apart.

Pot still whiskey is unique to Ireland and is a whiskey made from a "beer", or wash, made up of malted barley and another grain – normally unmalted barley, but occasionally wheat. This mix produces an oilier, earthier style of spirit. Pot still whiskey is almost always triple distilled to produce a spirit that is smoother and rounder than Scotch, because the extra spell of interaction between spirit and copper removes a higher proportion of congeners. It is also stronger and is reduced before bottling.

The fourth style of Irish whiskey, and the most famous, is blended Irish, a mix of pot still, grain and occasionally single malt. Jameson, Bushmills and Powers are the most famous of such whiskeys.

The distilleries

Ireland has only three major distilleries (plus one micro-distillery), though it produces around 30 different whiskeys. The bad news is that you can't visit two of the main distilleries – a pity because they're the plants where the art of Irish whiskey making is best demonstrated. The exception is Bushmills, a beautiful and friendly distillery in Antrim on Northern Ireland's rugged coastline. It's the nearest Ireland gets to making whiskey like the Scots, because here they make single malt. Ireland does have a number of whiskey tourist

Redbreast pot still whiskey

Green Spot pot still whiskey

**Powers
whiskey**

centres to visit too, but they are effectively museums – silent distilleries, populated with ghosts and a touch of sadness; memorials to an era when Irish whiskey swept the world before it. It's not that they are not worth visiting. It's just that – once you've seen the still waterways where the whiskey travelled off to Dublin and Belfast, peered inside silent stills, and marvelled at the engineering – well, it makes you want a glass of Ireland's finest.

Midleton

A few miles away from Cork, in the south of the Republic of Ireland, is Midleton. It is the main producer of Irish whiskey and the centre for Irish Distillers, owners of most Irish brands. It is also one of the most impressive distilleries in the world.

It's actually two distilleries on the same site. The old one – now a visitor centre and re-christened the Jameson Heritage Centre – is kept in immaculate condition, so that you can all but see the distillery workers who would have bustled through its spacious rooms before it closed down some 30 years ago. The new distillery, hidden away behind trees, is the whiskey equivalent of one of those vast industrial bases that James Bond stumbles into when trying to stop Blofeld destroying the world. Here, column stills and pot stills sit side by side on a massive scale and in high-tech splendour.

By employing a variety of combinations between the two distillation methods (continuous distillation in the column stills and batches of malt distilled in the pot stills), Midleton can, and does, produce more than 25 different spirits. Every production variable –

Midleton Very Rare is one of Ireland's most expensive blends.

from mash to fermentation, style of distillation, spirit flow and cut – is under the control of the master distiller, who can tweak things to make a diverse range of whiskey styles for different brands.

Bushmills

Just a few miles from the Giant's Causeway, in what is a spectacular part of the United Kingdom, stands Bushmills. Like a once-great football team that still commands a large and loyal following but has drifted from the Premier League and never quite found its way back, Bushmills is doing okay but really ought to be doing a whole lot better.

Bushmills 16-year-old single malt whiskey

However, it was sold to drinks giant Diageo a few years ago, so perhaps it will now get the support and exposure it so richly deserves. And there are already signs that its malt and its excellent blend, Black Bush, are being promoted more energetically.

Bushmills is a triple distilled single malt. This straightaway creates a problem, because its distilling costs are 50 per cent higher than those of its cousins just a short distance to the east in Scotland. High

Bushmills Distillery

A spirit safe at Bushmills

Cooley's warehouse at the old Locke's Distillery, Kilbeggan

want to know more?

further reading
• 1000 Years of Irish Whiskey by Malachy Magee
• The Whiskeys of Ireland by Peter Mulryan

weblink
www.visting
distilleries.com

energy prices make that difference considerable. But Bushmills doesn't shirk its responsibilities when it comes to quality, and the distillery invests in the finest casks, too, including some outstanding sherry casks. If you're in the mood to spend a bit, go for the wonderful Bushmills 16-year-old. If not, try Black Bush, a blend with about 80 per cent malt content and a wonderful example of the art of Irish blending at its very best.

Cooley
Cooley is an independent distillery, situated north of Dublin on the Cooley Peninsula, not far from Northern Ireland. The distillery operates from an ugly former industrial alcohol plant, but Cooley has been an exciting addition to the Irish scene. It has resurrected some traditional whiskey names and is experimenting with a range of styles. Particularly noteworthy are its Connemara 12-year-old and Connemara cask strength whiskeys, both of which are peated single malts.

Kilbeggan
The village of Kilbeggan used to be home to Locke's Distillery *(see opposite)*. That distillery fell silent in 1953, but Cooley began leasing its warehouses for maturing their whiskeys a few years ago, and, as part of the celebrations for Locke's 250-year anniversary, Cooley began distilling again at Kilbeggan. Only the second distillation takes place on site at present, with the low wines being brought over from the main Cooley Distillery, but there are plans to put in a wash still soon. In the meantime, Kilbeggan produces about 325 litres of spirit a day.

Tourist centres

In addition to the Jameson Heritage Centre in Midleton and Bushmills, Ireland offers the whiskey enthusiast a number of other whiskey centres to visit.

• Tullamore

Bury Quay, Tullamore, County Offaly

00 353 57 932 5015; www.tullamore-dew.org

Tullamore Dew is produced under licence in Midleton, while the original distillery that first produced it is now a functional and pleasant enough whiskey museum.

• Old Jameson Distillery

Bow Street Distillery, Smithfield, Dublin

00 353 1 807 2369; www.oldjamesondistillery.com

This well-kept site will give you a solid grounding in the Jameson story and offers a guide to the Irish whiskey-making process.

• Locke's Distillery

Kilbeggan, County Westmeath

00 353 0506 32 134

For a long time, this was the Marie Celeste of the whiskey world, and the distillery still looks as though it has been transported perfectly from another era, so complete is it. Cooley started up the stills again at Kilbeggan in 2007, and the fact that it was so readily made functional again is testament to some amazing wood and iron engineering. A museum here explores the whiskey-making process, with a tour of some historic equipment, much of which dates back to the 18th century.

Tullamore Dew

Locke's whiskey was resurrected by Cooley to honour the old distillery at Kilbeggan.

THE MINE TO THE HOLLOW HAPPY BIRTHDAY JACK JACK DANIEL

THE BELLE OF LINCOLN

9 American whiskey

The whiskeys of America are related to those of Scotland in so much as they are made using only grain, yeast and water. But that's a little like suggesting that soccer and American football are similar because they are both played by two teams on a pitch with a ball. Beyond the basic ingredients, in every way that American whiskey can differ from Scotch, it does. From the spelling of the word "whiskey" – the Americans normally, but not always, use the form with an "e" – to the way the spirit is distilled and matured, American whiskey is a very different beast.

What is American whiskey?

Metaphorically speaking, American whiskey is like its football – all big padding and helmets. Some would say that it lacks subtlety and sophistication, but those with a taste for it very often find Scotch unapproachable. American whiskey is also, somewhat surprisingly, a misunderstood category.

Jack Daniel's Tennessee whiskey

Jim Beam Kentucky bourbon

Ridgemount Reserve from Kentucky's Barton Distillery

American whiskey styles

Outside of the States, it's a relatively small number of people who know much about American whiskey, and although many will have heard the term applied to the most ubiquitous American whiskey – the style known as bourbon (and pronounced "ber-bun") – it's unlikely that many could name three different brands.

Not all American whiskeys are bourbons. Indeed, the most famous American whiskey, and one of the biggest selling spirits on the planet, Jack Daniel's, isn't a bourbon. It is ruled out on a technicality, and actually comes under the designation of "Tennessee whiskey". Jim Beam is a bourbon, but in its most basic form, the standard white label version, it is an adequate but unexceptional representation of the style. To draw a Scottish analogy, it's more of a Bell's than an aged Laphroaig.

But bourbon is an important whiskey in global, not just national, terms. Some of the foremost drinks writers argue that, overall, America maintains the highest calibre of production in the world. The American whiskey sector is small but almost perfectly formed, and some of its whiskeys are capable of going head to head with Scotland's very best.

American whiskey and bourbon

While all bourbons are American whiskeys, not all American whiskeys are bourbons. There are distilleries throughout the United States that make whiskey in other styles and employ different methods, including those that use malted barley and distil their spirit in pot stills, much as things are done in Scotland.

George Dickel Tennessee whisky (spelt without an "e")

The most notable non-bourbon whiskey is Jack Daniel's, and it serves to illustrate how strict the rules are governing bourbon production. Jack Daniel's is made in Tennessee in pretty much the exact manner as bourbon whiskey. However, before it is put into the barrel after distillation, it is passed through a wall of maple wood charcoal. This procedure, known as the Lincoln County Process, helps remove fats and congeners, and makes the spirit smoother. But it is strictly forbidden under the rules governing the production of bourbon. So, like the other Tennessee distillery, that of George Dickel, Jack is excluded. Quite happily, we might add, because down in Tennessee they're pretty confident that they are making a better product anyway.

must know

America's top distilleries include:

- Barton Brands
- Buffalo Trace
- Four Roses
- George Dickel
- Heaven Hill
- Jack Daniel's
- Jim Beam
- Maker's Mark
- Wild Turkey
- Woodford Reserve

Woodford Reserve Distillery

The Lincoln County Process of charcoal mellowing the whiskey

**The industrial-scale
Jim Beam Distillery**

Heaven Hill's visitor centre

must know
Bourbon whiskey takes
its name from Bourbon
County in Kentucky,
which in turn takes its
name from the French
royal house of Bourbon.
During America's War
of Independence, the
French supported
"rebel colonists", and
so Bourbon County
was named as an act
of gratitude.

A few hours north of the Jack Daniel's home in
Lynchburg is the state of Kentucky. While you don't
have to come from Kentucky to make bourbon, it
helps. America's greatest distilling names are
grouped in a concentrated area that extends around
the state capital of Louisville (the home town of
Muhammed Ali) and stretches down to bourbon's
capital, Bardstown. The distilleries based here
include Jim Beam, Wild Turkey, Heaven Hill, Buffalo
Trace, Maker's Mark, Woodford Reserve, Barton
Brands and Four Roses.

Kentucky casts a huge shadow over the rest of
America's whiskey producers, as does bourbon. So
for the purposes of this book that's where we'll focus.

Making bourbon

At its most simplistic, the process of making bourbon
mirrors that of making single malt Scotch. You start
with grain, make a wash, ferment it with yeast, distil
it and then mature it in oak barrels. In practice,
though, bourbon is bound by very different rules and
is produced by a very different process. Single malt
Scotch can be made using just one grain – malted
barley. Bourbon can be made with a mix of grains, the
dominant one of which is corn. At least 51% of the

mix has to be corn by law. Normally, but not always, the mix of grains will be made up with two others. Usually some malted barley will be used because it is the best grain for providing the base for the conversion of sugars and enzymes into alcohol. But unmalted barley, wheat and rye are also used.

Woodford Reserve's pot stills

Distilling bourbon

The processes of creating a grist (the ground grain), fermentation and making the wash are similar to those for producing Scotch malt whisky. But the distillation process in most bourbon-producing distilleries is different. Instead of a batch of wash being distilled in a pot still, the wash is produced continuously, with distillation taking place in a column still, where the wash is forced down over steam at very high pressure and temperature.

There's nothing very pretty about a column still and – with the exception of Woodford Reserve, where pot stills are used, and Maker's Mark, which is maintained as if it were a museum – bourbon distilleries can be ugly, industrial places.

That doesn't mean there is anything second-rate about the spirit they produce. Such distilleries can produce a high volume of top-quality spirit, which comes off the stills at a much higher alcoholic strength than Scottish single malt spirit.

must know

Bourbon must be aged in new white oak barrels for a minimum of two years. This may seem quite a short time, but maturation in Kentucky happens much faster than in the generally cooler climes of Scotland.

Maturing bourbon

The real magic of bourbon is in the maturation phase. Unlike in Scotland, where casks that are used have previously contained something else, in America only new casks made of American white oak can be used. In fact, the very reason for Scotland

Fermenting tanks at Brown-Forman Distillery

must know
There is a subtlety to burning the barrels used for maturing bourbon, and several levels of charring are employed to vary the effects upon the spirit. The heaviest charring releases the deepest tannins and vanillins in the oak.

importing so many cheap whiskey barrels from Kentucky and Tennessee is because there's an abundance of redundant barrels from the bourbon trade. Before it is used for bourbon maturation, the barrel is charred, or toasted, on the inside so that the spirit can more easily interract with the oak.

Once the whiskey is filled into the barrel, it is stored for maturation. Here, too, Kentucky is at odds with Scotland. Huge multi-floored warehouses, each like a small block of flats, are used. And, this being Kentucky, the warehouses bake in high summer temperatures and are at the mercy of the harsh bitter winds that sweep from the Appalachian Mountains during the short but very sharp winter. The temperature contrast in Kentucky is extreme, from sub-zero to the high 30s celsius, and in summer temperatures can easily climb above 40 degrees.

Each floor of the warehouses can vary from three to five degrees, producing "honeypot" areas, where maturation is at its best. The overall effect of such temperature variation is to put maturation in Kentucky on fast-forward. In Scotland, there is a dignified and stately maturation period. In Kentucky, the liquid's temperature rises and falls more dramatically than Wall Street during a mortgage crisis. The maturing spirit expands and contracts, accordingly, soaking deep into the wood, then shrinking back from it. The wood rapidly adds flavour and colour to the spirit, and removes fats and congeners to dramatic effect.

Traditional wooden fermenting vats at Woodford Reserve

The results of maturation

The reaction between wood and spirit produces rich fruit and vanillery notes that are instantly recognisable as bourbon. A sweet, burnt toffee character is very typical of bourbon, combined with a medley of flavours that might include confectionery, saddle polish and rich cherry fruit cake.

While maturation in Scotland must take place for a minimum of three years, in Kentucky it is two. And while, as a rough guide, single malt whisky reaches its best somewhere between 12 and 18 years, bourbon is seen to achieve its premium age between six and nine years. An indication of just how different the maturation process is in Kentucky, when compared to Scotland, is provided by the alcoholic strength of the spirit before it enters the barrel and when it comes out. In Scotland, the spirit will evaporate during maturation, and the strength will decline slightly each year. In Kentucky, the opposite is true. The matured whiskey is actually stronger than the spirit that was first put into the barrel.

Jim Beam bourbon barrels in storage during maturation

Seeking out good bourbon

Even the mainstream brands of bourbon are made to an extremely high quality, and Jim Beam, Bulleit, Buffalo Trace and Wild Turkey all have much to

Woodford Reserve bourbon

Maker's Mark bourbon

recommend them. The following bourbons, however, are suggestions for anyone wishing to explore the category more seriously:

Premium bourbons

• Maker's Mark: The gentlest of bourbons, due to its higher than normal wheat content. Smooth, rounded and a great introduction to bourbon.

• Woodford Reserve: At the other end of the bourbon spectrum is this classic, packed with punchy spice notes from the higher than average rye content.

• Wild Turkey 101: The 101 refers to the strength, being the American proof level, equivalent to 50.5% abv. Seen as the real bourbon drinker's bourbon, Wild Turkey sells well at rodeos.

• Four Roses: An easy to drink and balanced bourbon that has started to receive the support it deserves.

• Knob Creek: A bold, assertive and rounded fruit punch of a bourbon, from the Jim Beam stable.

Four Roses small-batch bourbon

Van Winkle 23-year-old bourbon

Super premium

• George T. Stagg: Notoriously difficult to find, but weighty, complex and as sophisticated as any whisky you'll find. It has a powerful punch too. Look out for a cask strength, which comes at over 60% ABV.

• Eagle Rare 17-year-old: Very old for a bourbon, but it's not destroyed by the wood. Indeed, the spice and oak are remarkably checked by the fruit and vanilla notes. A classic!

• Pappy Van Winkle 23-year-old: Van Winkle specialise in very old bourbon, and nothing from the stable is anything less than great. This is a monster.

• William Lerue Weller: Wheat is a key ingredient to this wonderful whiskey from the Sazerac stable.

Other American whiskey styles

While by law bourbon requires a mash containing 51% corn, it is possible to make other styles of whiskey by varying the kinds of grain in the mash bill. One of the most underrated styles of whiskey, for instance, and one that is having something of a resurgence, is rye whiskey. It's still not easy to find, but Rittenhouse Rye, from Heaven Hill, is a good starting point; Van Winkle Family Reserve Rye 13-year-old is like going three rounds with Muhammed Ali; and Sazerac Rye is a world-class whiskey, both in its youthful guise (as a 6-year-old) or in its full 18-year-old maturity.

Rittenhouse rye whisky

Wheat whiskey has also re-emerged in recent years, the best example being Bernheim Original Straight Wheat Whiskey, from Heaven Hill.

Visiting Kentucky

Every year in mid-September, Kentucky hosts a bourbon festival in Bardstown. For four or five days, the small town comes alive with events, including a cigar and whiskey evening, a bourbon racing night and a grand gala attended by the great and the good of Kentucky, at which every distillery puts on a lavish display of style and opulence.

If you get the weather – and you normally do – this is the perfect time to wallow in bourbon's glory, to watch the barrel races and to visit local attractions such as the Oscar Getz Bourbon Museum.

want to know more?
• Some distilleries offer tours of their whiskey-making facilities and have reasonable visitor centres. The best of them all is the recently built visitor attraction at Heaven Hill Distillery.

further reading
• The Bourbon Companion: The Connoisseurs' Guide by Gary Regan and Mardee Haidin Regan
• Bardstown: Hospitality, History and bourbon by Dixie Hibbs
• Classic Bourbon, Tennessee and Rye Whiskey by Jim Murray
• Bourbon Straight: The uncut and Unfiltered Story of American Whiskey by Charles K Cowdrey

10 The rest of the world

Although this book mainly focuses on Scottish single malts, it does include chapters on Ireland and America, too, as the main styles of whisky come from these three countries. To a great extent, whisky produced elsewhere emulates that produced by one of these countries – in most cases, Scotland. But that isn't the full picture, and there are other whisky-producing territories that deserve consideration.

Current trends

Canada has played a major role in the development of whisky and has its own unique style. It has been in decline for some years now but its influence is still considerable. Japan is on the opposite trajectory. After a long gestation period, its whiskies now have a distinctive Japanese style and are being widely lauded.

Canada's Glenora Distillery

Canadian Club whisky   **Canadian Mist whisky**

Canadian whisky

The Canadian whisky industry is like a former heavyweight boxer seeing out his twilight years, and now the glorious champion of yesteryear is struggling to survive. Nearly all Canada's principal whisky brands are under foreign ownership, and the few exceptions rarely make it over the border into the USA, let alone further afield.

Yet Canadian whisky, as we know it today, has a history stretching back to the mid-19th century. Following the introduction of the column still and continuous distillation in the 1830s, distilleries sprang up across the country. And during the country's golden period in the first half of the 20th century, the mammoth companies of Hiram Walker and Seagram not only stood proud in North America, but also dominated the entire whisky world.

Canada perfected a whisky style of its own, too, based around rye. Unlike American rye – where spicy and bold rye dominates a mash normally made of three grains – Canadian whisky blended corn-based spirit with a large number of different ryes produced in complex distilleries using different fermentations, spirit runs and distillations. And, under Canadian rules, a small amount of other whisky could also be added to the mix. The resulting whiskies were smooth, rounded and easy to drink. But they were more than that – they were highly complex, sophisticated and brilliantly balanced too.

Good examples of this style of whisky can still be found today, and a journey to Canada with a good guide book can still pay dividends.

Canadian whisky's problem has partly been down to its success in the cocktail sector. For, like a soap opera actor who stays in a part too long, Canadian whisky has become typecast – saddled with a reputation only for mixing.

Today, the country's distilleries are dispersed across the vast expanse of Canada. Canadian Club is produced at Walkerville, Ontario and Canadian Mist is also produced in Ontario, at Georgian Bay. Crown Royal is produced at Gimli Distillery in Manitoba. The future for Canada, however, might lie with a small wave of newish distilleries that are trying to do something a little bit different. In Nova Scotia, Glenora Distillery is producing a Scottish style single

Canadian Club Reserve   **Crown Royal whisky**

Canadian Mist's stainless-steel fermenters

Pot stills at Japan's
Yamazaki Distillery

Yoichi Distillery

Ichiro Akuto's
Card Series
whisky

Suntory's Hibiki
17-year-old

Nikka Black
Pure Malt

Karuizawa
17-year-old
single cask

malt whisky, using imported barley and genuine pot stills. Kittling Ridge in Ontario is in the process of creating a breed of "New World" Canadian whiskies, and, on Vancouver Island, Winchester Cellars is at a very early stage of creating its own whisky.

Can the old champ bounce back and be a contender again after so long? We shall see.

Japanese whisky

While Canadian whisky reached for the stars for a while before crashing spectacularly back to earth, Japanese whisky for a long time struggled to get off the ground at all, bumping along over the decades to no great effect. But the country has been producing whisky for the better part of a century now, and, in recent years, has begun to reap the rewards of all the hard work and practice; since 2000, Japan has released a number of truly world-class whiskies.

Whisky production in Japan was started by Shinjiro Torii and Masataka Taketsuru. Taketsuru had worked in distilleries in Scotland, and he realised that parts of Japan provided the perfect environment for whisky production. The first distillery was Yamazaki, situated between Osaka and Kyoto. Taketsuru was responsible for Japan's second distillery too, after he left Yamazaki Distillery and identified what he thought would be the perfect location to set up his own distillery, Yoichi, on Japan's most northerly island, Hokkaido. Taketsuru's company became Nikka and Torii's company, based at the Yamazaki Distillery, was later renamed Suntory. To this day Suntory and Nikka account for more than 80% of Japan's whisky output.

Yamazaki 25-year-old   **Kirin Fuji Distillery**

It's only in recent years that any Japanese whisky has travelled across the world, but Japan is now doing for whisky what it has done for cars – studying, emulating and eventually equalling, if not surpassing, the best products made elsewhere.

The Japanese whisky industry has had to overcome some hefty problems. If there has been a snobbishness from the West towards Japanese whisky, then it has suffered the same difficulty two-fold on its home turf, where Scotch whisky is revered. Added to this is the Japanese work culture, in which it is traditionally not acceptable for rival companies to interact with each other. Whereas Scottish distillers share malts with each other for their blends, in Japan traditionally no such arrangement has existed. Therefore, for Japanese distilleries to produce blends, they have either had to produce a range of whiskies themselves or bring in Scottish malt, undermining the whole concept of a unique Japanese whisky style.

Japan stayed in the shadows until about 10 years ago. Even as recently as 2000, a book on world whisky by an acclaimed drinks writer didn't see fit to mention the country at all. That's all changing now though – and fast. Championed by the likes of

must know

10 of the best Japanese whiskies to try:

- Fuji Gotemba 15-year-old
- Gimko Vatted Malt
- Hakushu 18-year-old
- Hibiki 17 Year Old
- Hokutu Suntory Pure Malt 12 Year Old
- Ichiro Single Cask Card Series
- Karuizawa Single Cask series
- Suntory Pure Malt 15 Year Old
- Yamazaki Vintage series
- Yoichi 10 Year Old

Michael Jackson, Jim Murray and most recently Dave Broom, Japanese whiskies have started to attract considerable interest from enthusiasts. A clutch of prizes – from attaining top score in the inaugural *Whisky Magazine* Best of the Best awards in 2001 to gaining two of the top five places in the 2007 World Whisky awards – has confirmed the quality.

Greater supply through Japanese-owned whisky companies, such as Morrison Bowmore, and from specialist suppliers, such as the Number One Drinks Company, have fired the imagination. And even the traditional rivalry within Japan itself has thawed. Senior officials from three companies shared a platform at Whisky Live in Tokyo a couple of years back, for instance, and a vatted malt called Gimko has, for the first time, included a mix of malts from more than one company.

Best of all from an enthusiast's point of view, the whiskies we're now tasting are not only of extraordinarily high quality, but they seem to be developing a distinctive mushroomy characteristic all of their own. It's something of an acquired taste, but, once you buy into it, it's the clearest proof yet that Japan is capable of producing whiskies that are far more than just copy-cat impersonators.

Unsurprisingly, most of the whisky making it over from Japan is the product of one of the two big companies, Suntory and Nikka. But it's worth seeking out whisky from Fuji-Gotemba, Karuizawa, and Ichiro Malts too. Japanese whiskies tend not to be cheap, but there is a growing band of whisky enthusiasts who find them every bit as exciting as those coming from Scotland or America. And plenty who believe that some of them are set to become major stars.

India's Amrut whisky

The rest of the world

Overall, the world of whisky is just like the world of rugby union: dominated by a handful of big players, with a number of also-rans occasionally rising above their status for a brief spell in the sun before fading away again. Or, at least, that's how it's been up until now. All that might yet change in the not too distant future, as demand for whisky – stimulated by new wealth in the old Slavic and Eastern bloc countries, coupled with rising demand in the emerging Asian markets – creates new opportunities.

A large number of countries are producing whiskies these days, and in some cases entirely new styles are being made. Weidenauer, in Austria, produces an oat whisky and a "Spelt" whisky, which uses a special strain of wheat. In France, Distillerie des Menhirs produces Eddu Gold and Eddu Silver, which is made with buckwheat (thereby flirting with the rules of whisky, as buckwheat isn't technically a grain). South Africa, Australia and New Zealand have all made significant contributions to the world of whisky too.

The inquisitive should try Penderyn from Wales, the cask-strength version of Amrut from India and the most recent Mackmyra Preludium from Sweden.

want to know more?
further reading
• **Complete Book of Whisky** by Jim Murray
• **The Whisky Bible** by Jim Murray
• **Encyclopaedia of Whisky** by Michael Jackson

Sullivans Cove whiskies from Tasmania

Australia's Bakery Hill malt

Wales's Penderyn malt

France's Eddu whisky

SINGLE MALT SCOTCH WHISKY
GLENKEIR TREASURES™
This Single Malt Scotch Whisky is exclusive to The Whisky Shop having been chosen after a rigorous search. We have uncovered a hidden treasure and supplies are extremely limited.
40%vol
50cl
PRODUCT OF SCOTLAND

11 Independent bottlers

Enter into one of the better whisky shops and it won't take you long to realise that the number of bottles on the shelves that have come directly from a distillery constitute only a fraction of the total number. Closer inspection will reveal companies with a range of bottles from several distilleries. Many will have unusual age statements and might highlight the year that the whisky was distilled or bottled. These are the products of independent bottlers, who have an important role in the whisky world, particularly for fanatics passionate about the produce of particular distilleries.

Industry mavericks

Official distillery bottlings are to whisky what official CD releases of a rock band are to music. And it follows that the releases from independent bottlers are the industry's "bootlegs" – unofficial releases that fans *must have*. Like bootlegs, their quality varies from utter gems to sub-standard versions of all-time classics.

Rosebank Distillery closed in 1993, but stocks of this Lowland malt are still released by independent bottlers such as Douglas Laing.

Limited releases

Every official bottle from a distillery is a careful marriage of casks, with the marriage designed to ensure that, no matter when or where the whisky is purchased, to all intents and purposes, it tastes the same. But most single malt whisky is produced to be used in blended whisky, and different distilleries swap malts so that each company has the widest selection from which to create its blends.

Inevitably, and particularly when whisky is in one of its ebb periods, some casks of malt become available on the open market, and it is these that the independent bottlers seize upon. Unlike the rounded and balanced mix of casks that the distillery's owner will put out officially, an independent bottler might get hold of just one, two or three casks at a time. The malt might have been aged for an unusual number of years, and, as each and every cask differs from the next, the whisky that ends up inside the bottle can differ markedly from what might be expected.

This is part of the appeal, of course. If a cask is going to yield only 250 to 300 bottles, a single cask bottling will be extremely limited. When it's gone, it's gone for ever, and that gives it considerable rarity value. If you buy an independent bottling from your favourite distillery, there is always the potential to find your perfect dram.

Rarity value or intrinsic value?

So, independent bottlings often have the frisson of their rarity, but the all-important question remains: are they any good?

For understandable reasons, the distillery owners tend to be rather suspicious of independent bottlers. Distilleries have no control over the quality of independent releases, and the distillery's good name is at stake. Some companies even add a small amount of whisky from another distillery to each cask going for blending, which ensures that it cannot be sold to an independent bottler as a single malt.

On the other hand, independents do provide cash flow for distilleries in bad times, and they have done much to stimulate excitement and interest in whisky by providing dynamism in the market.

Independent bottlers tend to buy a small number of casks at a time from any one distillery, hence their bottlings are limited and, if good, acquire a rarity value.

Age statements on independent bottlings may be unusual. In this case, Glenkeir Treasures has released a 9-year-old Ledaig from Tobermory Distillery.

Some independent bottlers, such as Gordon & MacPhail, put a great deal of effort into maturing whisky until it is at its very best before bottling.

At worst, whiskies released in this way can be horrendous, and the buyer needs to be aware of unscrupulous operators who are prepared to sell anything, whatever the quality. The easiest way to avoid them is to look to the established companies, whose reputations have been built on the back of the whiskies they sell under their name. A little bit of research and advice helps too. *Whisky Magazine*, for example, runs an "independent bottlers' challenge" every year, in which medals are awarded following a succession of blind tastings.

Once you've discovered a distillery that you love, this sort of effort to seek out independent releases is certainly worthwhile. It's whisky's equivalent of opening oysters in search of pearls: fun, exciting and potentially very rewarding.

Supermarkets and other outlets

Supermarkets, some whisky retailers and a whole host of tourist outlets, particularly in Scotland, have their own whiskies. Many of these are very good indeed. Unlike some of the tosh that is bottled under the name "blended Scotch whisky", any bottle

The Whisky Shop, London

bearing the words "Scottish single malt whisky" will be 100% malt whisky from one of Scotland's distilleries, and it will have been supplied officially.

Such is the competition between the supermarkets that considerable effort is put into sourcing good quality malt. If you enjoy a tipple but don't want to dip into your better single malts too often, the High Street retailers might be worth exploring.

Dedicated independent stores and groups, such as The Whisky Shop, are often bottlers as well. Some of them have become well established in their own right. Glenkeir Treasures, Royal Mile Whiskies, Loch Fyne Whiskies and Queen of the Moorlands in the UK, La Maison du Whisky in France, and Park Avenue Liquors in New York are all rich hunting grounds for dedicated enthusiasts.

want to know more?

Here is a selection of the best independent bottlers:
- Berry Bros & Rudd (www.bbr.com)
- Cadenhead (www.wmcaden head.com)
- Dewar Rattray (www.dewarrattray.com)
- Douglas Laing (www.douglaslaing.com)
- Duncan Taylor (www.dtcscotch.com)
- Gordon & MacPhail (www.gordonand macphail.com)
- Ian MacLeod (www.ianmacleod.com)
- Murray McDavid (www.murray-mcdavid.com)
- Signatory (www.totalbeverage solution.com)
- Scottish Malt Whisky Society (www.smws.co.uk)
- www.whisky-distilleries.net publishes information about many independent bottlers

Glossary

abv

see alcohol by volume

Age

The number of years whisky has been in the cask. On a label, the age refers to the youngest whisky in the bottle.

Ageing

The process of maturing whisky in the cask.

Alcohol by volume

The alcoholic strength of a drink expressed as a percentage of the liquid overall. It is usually abbreviated to abv.

Angels' share

Term given to the whisky that evaporates from the cask during the period of maturation.

Beer

Product of adding yeast to the wort or mash, and also known as wash.

Blended malt whisky

Confusing modern term for vatted malts – a mix of malt whiskies from different distilleries.

Blended whisky

A mix of malt whiskies and grain whisky.

Bond warehouse

Where whisky is stored until excise duty is paid.

Bourbon

American style of whisky made from a mash of at least 51% corn, distilled to a strength of no more than 80% abv and then matured in charred new American oak barrels for at least two years.

Brewing

Process of turning a grain and water solution (mash) into beer (wash) by adding yeast and producing alcohol and carbon dioxide.

Caramel

Caramel is sometimes added to whisky to provide a consistency of colour from one batch to another. It is not intended to impart any flavour, but experts will tell you otherwise.

Cask strength whisky

Whisky that is bottled at the strength it comes out of the cask (typically 57–63% abv) as opposed to the diluted 40–46% strength at which most whiskies are bottled.

Charcoal filtering

The process of dribbling new make spirit through a wall of charcoal, used by some US distilleries. *See also the Lincoln County Process.*

Charring

Firing of the inside of a barrel to create an environment that will impart flavour to the spirit which comes into contact with it.

Chill-filtration

Impurities or congeners in whisky make it go cloudy when it is cold or if water is added. They can be removed, however, by chilling the whisky and passing it through cardboard filters. There has been a trend away from chill-filtering, though, because it is believed that the impurities contribute to the whisky's overall taste.

Clearic
Whiskymakers' name for new make spirit.

Coffey stills
See Continuous distillation

Column stills
See Continuous distillation

Condensers
The equipment that turns spirit vapour back to liquid – normally copper pipes surrounded by cold water.

Congeners
The name of the scores of organic chemicals in the distilled spirit. Many have to be separated from the final whisky because they are poisonous, taste horrible, or both.

Continuous distillation
The process of commer-cially making grain spirit by forcing the wash over steam under high pressure. The process can produce large quantities of high-strength spirit.

Copper
The metal that's most used in distillation. Copper removes sulphury and vegetal aromas, and other impurities.

Distilling
The process of heating alcohol to separate it from water.

Doubler
A second still sometimes added to the continuous distillation process.

Draff
Spent grains that remain after mashing, which are dried and packaged off as non-alcoholic cattle feed.

Dram
Scottish term for a small measure of whisky.

Drum malting
Commercial method of turning barley into malt.

Enzymes
Catalysts in grain which help the conversion of starches into alcohol by making them fermentable when mixed with yeast.

Feints
The final portion of spirit produced in the second

distillation. It is too poor to keep and is recycled for redistillation. Feints are also know as tails.

Foreshots
See Heads

Grain whisky
Whisky made from one or more grains, such as corn, wheat or unmalted barley. Grain whisky is made using continuous distillation, and a small amount of malted barley is used in the process to aid fermentation.

Grist
A rough flour made by crushing the grain. When added to hot water, it forms the mash.

Heads
The first portion of alcohol collected during second distillation. It is rejected and recycled for redistillation because, at best, the spirit tastes unpleasant and, at worst, is poisonous. Heads are also known as foreshots.

High wines
A mix of once-distilled spirit and the rejected

spirit from the second distillation. It has an abv percentage in the high 20s and goes on for a second distillation.

Hogsheads
Remade, or dump, hogsheads are American bourbon barrels that have been taken apart, shipped to Scotland, and remade using a proportion of new staves and new heads to give them a capacity of 250 litres – bigger than the original 200-litre barrels. Hogsheads are the most common type of cask used in Scotland .

Irish pot still whiskey
A mix of malted and unmalted barley distilled in a copper still in Ireland.

Kilning
The heating of germinating barley to stop it developing further and turn it into malt.

Leaching
American term for the charcoal mellowing process that's used in the production of some US whiskeys.

Lincoln County Process
A method of filtering used in Tennessee, whereby new make spirit is poured through Maplewood charcoal to filter out undesirable flavours.

Liquor
Name for the hot water in the mashing process.

Low wines
Name given to the spirit produced from the first distillation. It has an alcoholic strength of about 23% abv and is mixed with the rejected spirit from the previous second distillation before it goes to the spirit still.

Lyne arm
The copper arm running from the top of the pot still to the condenser. The lyne arm's size, distance from the base of the still and angle of incline will all affect the final spirit.

Malt
Grain that has been tricked into germinating using moisture and warmth, then kilned to halt the germination.

Most often the grain is barley, but rye can be malted too.

Mash
The mix of grist with hot water. The sweet liquid that results from the mash is called wort.

Mash bill
American term for the percentage of each grain used to make whiskey.

Mash tun
Vessel where grist and hot water are mixed.

Nose
The aroma of a whisky.

Nosing
The process of assessing a whisky by smelling it.

Peated malt
Whisky made with a percentage of malted barley that has been dried over a peat fire and which takes on its smoky and phenolic characterisitics.

Pot stills
Copper kettles used for distilling in batches. They come in myriad shapes and sizes, and these variations have an affect on the whisky's flavour.

Quaich

Two-handled drinking vessel for sharing whisky.

Reflux

Process by which heavier spirit fails to reach the lyne arm near the top of the still and runs back into the still. When reflux is high, only the lightest spirits are recondensed and a light whisky is produced. In shorter, more squat stills, reflux is low, resulting in a heavier, oilier spirit.

Rummager

A device sometimes used in pot stills to agitate the liquid so as to prevent any solids from burning from direct heat.

Rye whiskey

Whiskey produced with a minimum of 51% rye in the mash bill.

Single malt whisky

Malt whisky is made from only malted barley, yeast and water. If it is a single malt, it is the product of just one distillery. It may contain whisky from lots of different casks, though.

Sour mash

In the production process a minimum of 25% of the mash must be made up of liquid left at the bottom of the still from the previous distillation. This is known as the "backset", and it's a liquid that has been stripped of alcohol and sugars. It's useful because it can kill harmful bacteria.

Spirit still

The still in which the final distillation takes place.

Still

The vessel used for distilling spirit. There are two main types: a pot still, used for batch distillation; and a continuous or column still, used for continuous distillation.

Stillage

American term for the residue at the bottom of a still which is stripped of alcohol and sugars. When the solids are removed the liquid left forms the "backset" to be recycled in the sour mash process.

Sweet mash

A mash to which no backset has been added.

Tails

See Feints

Vatting

The mixing of malts from different distilleries. Vatted malts are now referred to as blended malt whiskies.

Wash

See beer

Wash still

First pot still used in distillation, producing a liquid with an abv of just over 20%.

Wort

See Mash

Worm

Coiled and horizontal copper tube immersed in cold water that is used to recondense the spirit vapours produced in distillation.

Yeast

Living micro-organism added to the mash to produce alcohol by feeding on the sugars in the mash.

Need to know more?

Further Reading

Magazines:

Whisky Magazine
St Faiths House
Mountergate, Norwich
NR1 1PY
England
01603 633808
www.whiskymag.com

The Malt Advocate
312 Main Street
Emmaus, PA 18049
USA
610 967 1083
www.maltadvocate.com

Books:

Complete Book of Whisky,
Jim Murray
(Carlton Books)

The Whisky Bible,
Jim Murray
(Carlton Books)

*Complete Guide to Single
Malt Whisky,*
Michael Jackson
(Running Press)

Malt Whisky Companion,
Michael Jackson
(Dorling Kindersley)

Scotland and its Whiskies,
Michael Jackson
(Duncan Baird Publishers)

Malt Whisky,
Charles MacLean
(Mitchell Beazley)

Handbook of Whisky,
Dave Broom
(Diane Publishing
Company)

*The Scottish Whisky
Distilleries,*
Misako Udo
(Black and White
Publishing)

Whisky Classified,
David Wishart
(Pavilion Books)

*Scotch Missed:
The Lost Distilleries
of Scotland,*
Brian Townsend
(Neil Wilson Publishing)

*1000 Years of
Irish Whiskey,*
Malachy Magee
(O'Brien Press Ltd)

The Whiskeys of Ireland,
Peter Mulryan
(O'Brien Press Ltd)

*The Bourbon Companion:
The Connoisseurs' Guide,*
Gary Regan and Mardee
Haidin Regan
(Running Press)

Organisations

The Scotch Malt
Whisky Society
The Vaults, 87 Giles Street
Edinburgh, EH6 6BZ
0131 554 3451
www.smws.com

The Scotch Whisky
Association
20 Atholl Crescent
Edinburgh, EH3 8HF
0131 222 9200
www.scotch-whisky.org.uk

Retailers

Loch Fyne Whiskies
Pitlochry
www.lfw.co.uk

Royal Mile Whiskies
Edinburgh and London
www.royalmile
whiskies.com

The Whisky Shop
outlets across the UK
www.whiskyshop.com

The Whisky Exchange
www.thewhisky
exchange.com

Websites

www.scotchwhisky.net
www.visitingdistilleries.com
www.maltwhiskytrail.com
www.maltmaniacs.org
www.thewhiskyguide.com

Acknowledgements

Picture credits

The publishers would also like to thank the following for their assistance with images:

A Smith Bowman, Allied Domecq, Amrut, Bacardi, Bakery Hill Distillery, Balmenach Distillery, Barton Brands Ltd, Beam Global Spirits & Wine, Benriach Distillery, Berry Brothers & Rudd Ltd, Bertrand, The Brown-Forman Corporation, Buffalo Trace, Burn Stewart Distillers Ltd, Campari, Chivas Brothers, Clear Creek Distillery, CL WorldBrands Ltd, Copper Fox Distillery, Cooley Distillery, Compass Box, Diageo, Eddu, The Edrington Group, Fortune Brands Inc, Four Roses Distillery, Glenora Distillery, George Dickel Distillery, Glenmorangie, Gilbeys, Hanyu Distillery (Ichiro Akuto), Heaven Hill Distilleries, Highland Park, Highland Distillers Plc, Highwood Distillery, Höhler, Hiram Walker & Sons, Inver House Distillers, Irish Distillers Group, Isle of Arran Distillers, John Dewar and Sons Ltd, Kirin Brewery Co, Kittling Ridge, Lark Distillery, Mackmyra Distillery, Des Menhirs, Morrison Bowmore Distillers Ltd, Mitchell & Son Wine Merchants Ltd, Nant Distillery, Nikka, The Owl, Penderyn Distillery, Pernod Ricard, Piedmont Distillers Inc, Sazerac Company, Smith's, Southern Distilleries Ltd, The Southern Distilling Company, Spencerfield Spirits, St George's Distillery, St George Spirits, Suntory, Takara Shuzo & Okura Ltd, Tasmania Distillery, Thai Beverage Public Company Ltd, Tobermory Distillery, United Distillers & Vintners Ltd, United Spirits, Van Winkle Whiskeys, Whyte and Mackay Ltd, William Grant and Sons, Winchester Cellars.

Photographs on pages 2, 14, 38, 44, 178: Michael Ellis. A special thanks to Christopher Maclean and Rebecca Laurance at The Whisky Shop, London, for their assistance in taking these photographs.

Index

a'bunadh 58, 140
Aberfeldy 57, 140
Aberlour 58, 140
age statements 46
Airigh Nam Beist 59
Allt-a-Bhainne 112
American whiskey
11, 23, 161–69
Ancient Reserve 84
anCnoc 96, 145
angels' share 35
Antiquary, The 108
Ardbeg 59, 140
Ardmore 112, 141
Arran Distillery
60, 141
Arran, Isle of 37
Arumaticus Fumosus
66
Asian whisky 177
Auchentoshan
61, 141
Auchroisk 62
Aultmore 113
Authenticus 66
Baillie Nicol Jarvie 147
Balblair 63, 141
Ballantine's 82,
129, 147
Balmenach 113
Balvenie 64, 141
Banff 131
barley 29
Bell's 69, 121
Ben Nevis 65
Ben Wyvis 131
BenRiach 66,
141, 142
Benrinnes 114
Benromach 67, 142
Black Bottle 147
Bladnoch 68
Blair Athol 69
blended malts 21

blended whisky
10, 19
bottle labels 46
bourbon 23, 162–68
bourbon casks 34
Bowmore 70, 142
Braeval 131
Brechin 134
Brora 132, 142
Bruichladdich
71, 142
Bunnahabhain
72, 142, 143
Bushmills 157
buying whisky
45–51
Campbeltown
37, 104
Canadian whisky
25, 172–74
Caol Ila 73, 143
Caoran Reserve 84
Caperdonach 132
Cardhu 74
cask finishing 49
cask strength
whisky 48
casks 28, 33–35
chill-filtering 47
Chivas Regal 105,
112, 147
Cigar Malt 77
Clan Denny Islay 149
closed distilleries
51, 55, 130–34
Clynelish 75, 143
Coleburn 132
collecting whisky 50
Compass Box 149
congeners 32, 47
Convalmore 132
Cooley Distillery
158
copper 32
Cornish Cyder
Company 137
Cragganmore
76, 143

Craigellachie 114
Curiositas 66
cut (distilling) 33
Cutty Sark 119
Daftmill 136
Dailuaine 115
Dallas Dhu 110, 132
Dalmore 77, 143
Dalwhinnie 78, 143
Deanston 115
Delmé-Evans,
William 116
Dewar's 114, 147
Dewar's World of
Whisky 57, 110
distillation 31
distilleries for visiting
55, 57–109
Doig, Charles 103
Douglas Laing 93
Drumguish 127
Dufftown 116
Eagle Rare 168
Edradour 79
Elegancia 99
European whisky 177
Famous Grouse
128, 147
Famous Grouse
Experience 93, 111
feints 33
fermentation 29
Fettercairn 80
Flora & Fauna range
Dufftown 116
Glen Spey 120
Glenlossie 118
Inchgower 121
Strathmill 127
foreshots 33
Four Roses 168
George T. Stagg 168
glasses 40, 41
Glen Albyn 132
Glen Deveron 124
Glen Elgin 118
Glen Flagler 132
Glen Garioch 85

Glen Grant 87
Glen Keith 133
Glen Mhor 133
Glen Moray 91, 144
Glen Ord 92
Glen Scotia 119
Glen Spey 120
Glenallachie 116
Glenburgie 117
Glencadam 81, 143
Glendronach 82
Glendullan 117
Glenesk 132
Glenfarclas 83
Glenfiddich 84, 144
Glenglassaugh 133
Glengoyne 86
Glengyle 104
Glengyle 136
Glenkeir Treasures 183
Glenkinchie 88
Glenlivet 89, 144
Glenlochy 133
Glenlossie 118
Glenmorangie
90, 144
Glenrothes 119,
144, 145
Glentauchers 120
Glenturret 93
Glenugie 133
Glenury Royal 133
Gordon & MacPhail
67, 87, 113
grain whisky 16
Hankey Bannister
148
Hazelburn 104, 135
Heart of Speyside
(whisky) 66
Hereditus Fumosus
66
Highland distilleries
54
Highland Park
94, 145
Highlands 37
Hillside 132

Imperial 133
Inchgower 121
Inchmurrin 123
independent bottlers
179
Indian whisky 177
Inverleven 133
Irish whiskey 11,
22, 23, 151–59
Islay 37
Islay distilleries 54
J&B 122, 127
Jameson, Old
Distillery 159
Japanese whisky
24, 174–76
Johnnie Walker
73, 74, 115, 121,
148, 149
Jura 37
Jura Distillery
95, 145
Kilbeggan 158
Kilchoman 136
Kildalton 59
Kilkerran 104
Kinclaith 133
Kininvie 121
Knob Creek 168
Knockando 122
Knockdhu 96, 145
labels (bottles) 46
Ladyburn 134
Lagavulin 97, 145
Laphroaig 98, 145,
146
Ledaig 107
Linkwood 122
Littlemill 134
Loch Dhu 124
Loch Fyne Whiskies
51, 183
Loch Lomond 123
Lochside 134
Locke's Distillery
159
Longmorn 123
Longrow 104

Lord of the Isles
(whisky) 59, 87
low wines 31
Lowlands 37
lyne arm 31
Macallan 99, 146
Macduff 124
Macnamara 148
Maker's Mark 168
malt whisky 16, 21,
27–35,
malting 29
Mannochmore 124
maps (Scotland's
distilleries) 54–55
mash tun 30
maturation 33
Midleton Distillery
156
Millburn 134
Miltonduff 125
Monkey Shoulder
149
Mortlach 125
Mull 37
Museum of Malt
111
non chill-filtering 47
North Port 134
nosing and tasting
39–43
oak 34
Oak Cross 149
Oban 100
Old Pulteney 101,
146
Old Rhosdhu 123
Orkney 37
peat 30
Peat Monster 149
Penderyn 137
Pittyvaich 134
Port Charlotte 136
Port Ellen 134
pot still whiskey 22
Provenance 1974 59
Pulteney 101
Rittenhouse Rye 169

Robert Burns
(whisky) 60
Rosebank 134
Royal Brackla 126
Royal Lochnagar
102
Royal Mile Whiskies
183
Royal Salute 148
rye whiskey 24, 169
Sassicaia 67
Sazerac Rye 169
Scapa 126, 146
Scotch Whisky
Heritage Centre
111
Scotland's distilleries
53–136
Scotland's distilleries
map 54
Scotland's distilleries
to visit 57–109
Scotland's whisky
regions 36
Serendipity 149
sherry casks 34
Skye 37
Solera Reserve 84
Speyburn 103
Speyside 37, 127
Speyside distilleries
55
Springbank
104, 135
St George's Distillery
137
St Magdalene 134
Strathisla 105
Strathmill 127
Superstition (whisky)
95
tails 33
Talisker 106, 146
Tamdhu 128
Tamnavulin 134
tasting whisky
39–43
Teaninch 128

Tennessee whiskey
24
Tobermory 107
Tokaji 67
Tomatin 108
Tomintoul
129, 146
Tormore 129
Tullamore 159
Tullibardine 109
Uigeadail
uisge beatha/
uisce beatha 11,
151, 152, 153
wash 31
wash still 31
water
whisky making 29
drinking whisky
10, 40
wheat whiskey 169
whisky
buying 45–51
making 28–35,
152–55
types 15–23
Whisky Exchange 51
Whisky Magazine 51,
60, 106, 176, 182
whisky regions 36
Whisky Shop, The
51, 183
Whyte & Mackay
148
Wild Turkey 168
William Grant 64,
121, 148
William Lerue Weller
168
Winkle, Pappy Van
168, 169
wood finishes 49
Woodford Reserve
168
World Whisky Awards
106
worts 30
yeast 29

☽ Collins need to know?

Look out for these recent titles in Collins' practical and accessible need to know? series.

Other titles in the series:

Antique Marks
Aquarium Fish
Birdwatching
Body Language
Buying Property in France
Buying Property in Spain
Calorie Counting
Card Games
Card Making
Chess
Children's Parties
Codes & Ciphers
Decorating
Detox
Digital Photography
DIY
Dog and Puppy Care

Dog Training
Downloading
Drawing & Sketching
Dreams
Fertility & Conception
First Aid
Food Allergies
Golf
Guitar
Horse and Pony Care
How to Lose Weight
Kama Sutra
Kings and Queens
Knots
Low GI/GL Diet
Mushroom Hunting
NLP

Outdoor Survival
Party Games
Pilates
Poker
Pregnancy
Property
Sleep
Speak French
Speak Italian
Speak Spanish
Stargazing
Watercolour
Weather Watching
Weddings
Wine
Woodworking
The World

Universe
Yoga
Zodiac Types

**To order any of these titles, please telephone 0870 787 1732 quoting reference 263H.
For further information about all Collins books, visit our website:
www.collins.co.uk**